Drugs, Women, and Justice: Roles of the Criminal Justice System for Drug-Affected Women

Drugs, Women, and Justice: Roles of the Criminal Justice System for Drug-Affected Women has been co-published simultaneously as *Women & Criminal Justice*, Volume 17, Numbers 2/3 2006.

D1528715

Monographic Separates from *Women & Criminal Justice*®

For additional information on these and other Haworth Press titles, including descriptions, tables of contents, reviews, and prices, use the QuickSearch catalog at http://www.HaworthPress.com.

Drugs, Women, and Justice: Roles of the Criminal Justice System for Drug-Affected Women, edited by James A. Swartz, PhD, Patricia O'Brien, PhD, and Arthur J. Lurigio, PhD (Vol. 17, No. 2/3, 2006). *The numbers of women offenders involved in the correctional system are quickly growing.* Drugs, Women, and Justice: Roles of the Criminal Justice System for Drug-Affected Women *gathers a distinguished group of researchers and policy analysts into one volume to explore the broad social and individual implications of current policy and practice pertaining to women in the criminal justice system. This valuable resource provides readers with a superb overview of the current state of knowledge and provides recommendations for new directions. Each top-notch chapter was originally presented at the Drugs, Women, and Justice symposium at the Jane Addams Substance Abuse Research Collaboration in 2005.*

Women and Domestic Violence: An Interdisciplinary Approach, edited by Lynette Feder, PhD (Vol. 10, No. 2, 1999). *"An excellent overview of the criminal-justice response to domestic violence and is the best critical overview of the topic in print." (Evan Stark, PhD, MSW, Director, Domestic Violence Training Project, New Haven, CT)*

The Criminalization of a Woman's Body, edited by Clarice Feinman, PhD (Vol. 3, No. 1/2, 1992). *"Addresses women's concerns worldwide about threats to their autonomy, privacy, and bodily integrity, focusing on the laws of various countries." (SciTech Book News)*

Drugs, Women, and Justice: Roles of the Criminal Justice System for Drug-Affected Women

James A. Swartz, PhD
Patricia O'Brien, PhD
Arthur J. Lurigio, PhD
Editors

Drugs, Women, and Justice: Roles of the Criminal Justice System for Drug-Affected Women has been co-published simultaneously as *Women & Criminal Justice*, Volume 17, Numbers 2/3 2006.

Routledge
Taylor & Francis Group
NEW YORK AND LONDON

First Published 2006 by
The Haworth Press, Inc.

Published in 2009 by Routledge
711 Third Avenue, New York, NY 10017
2 Park Square, Milton Park, Abingdon, Oxfordshire OX14 4RN

First issued in paperback 2014

Routledge is an imprint of the Taylor & Francis Group, an informa business

Drugs, Women, and Justice: Roles of the Criminal Justice System for Drug-Affected Women has been co-published simultaneously as *Women & Criminal Justice*, Volume 17, Numbers 2/3 2006.

The development, preparation, and publication of this work has been undertaken with great care. However, the publisher, employees, editors, and agents of The Haworth Press and all imprints of The Haworth Press, Inc., including The Haworth Medical Press® and Pharmaceutical Products Press®, are not responsible for any errors contained herein or for consequences that may ensue from use of materials or information contained in this work. With regard to case studies, identities and circumstances of individuals discussed herein have been changed to protect confidentiality. Any resemblance to actual persons, living or dead, is entirely coincidental.

The Haworth Press is committed to the dissemination of ideas and information according to the highest standards of intellectual freedom and the free exchange of ideas. Statements made and opinions expressed in this publication do not necessarily reflect the views of the Publisher, Directors, management, or staff of The Haworth Press, Inc., or an endorsement by them.

Library of Congress Cataloging-in-Publication Data

Drugs, women, and justice : roles of the criminal justice system for drug-affected women / James A. Swartz, Patricia O'Brien, Arthur J. Lurigio, editors.
     p. cm.
     "Co-published simultaneously as Women & criminal justice, volume 17, numbers 2/3 2006."
     Papers presented at a symposium on "Drugs, Women, and Justice: a Research Perspective" sponsored by the Jane Addams College of Social Work in September 2005.
     Includes bibliographical references and index.

     1. Women–Drug use–United States. 2. Women prisoners–United States. 3. Female offenders–Rehabilitation–United States. 4. Drug addicts–Rehabilitation–United States. 5. Prisoners' families–United States. 6. Criminal justice, Administration of–United States. I. Swartz, James, 1955- II. O'Brien, Patricia, 1955- III. Lurigio, Arthur J. IV. Women & criminal justice.

HV5824.W6D794 2007
364.3'8–dc22
                                                2007018387

ISBN13: 978-1-138-86752-9 (pbk)
ISBN13: 978-0-7890-3624-7 (hbk)

The HAWORTH PRESS *Inc*

Abstracting, Indexing & Outward Linking

PRINT *and* ELECTRONIC BOOKS & JOURNALS

This section provides you with a list of major indexing & abstracting services and other tools for bibliographic access. That is to say, each service began covering this periodical during the the year noted in the right column. Most Websites which are listed below have indicated that they will either post, disseminate, compile, archive, cite or alert their own Website users with research-based content from this work. (This list is as current as the copyright date of this publication.)

Abstracting, Website/Indexing Coverage . . . . Year When Coverage Began

- **Expanded Academic ASAP (Thomson Gale)** 1998
- **Expanded Academic ASAP–International (Thomson Gale)** . . 1998
- **InfoTrac Custom (Thomson Gale)** 2006
- **InfoTrac OneFile (Thomson Gale)** 1998
- **Social Services Abstracts (ProQuest CSA)**
  <http://www.csa.com> 1991
- **Social Work Abstracts (NASW)**
  <http://www.silverplatter.com/catalog/swab.htm> 1991
- **Sociological Abstracts (ProQuest CSA)**
  <http://www.csa.com> 1991
- *Alternative Press Index (Print, online & CD-ROM from NISC)*
  <http://www.altpress.org> 2006
- *Cambridge Scientific Abstracts (now ProQuest CSA)*
  <http://www.csa.com> 2006
- *Contemporary Women's Issues (Thomson Gale)* 1998
- *Criminal Justice Abstracts (Sage & CSA)* 1991
- *Criminal Justice Periodicals (ProQuest CSA)*
  <http://www.proquest.com> 1993
- *Current Abstracts (EBSCO)* <http://search.ebscohost.com> 2007
- *Current Citations Express (EBSCO)*
  <http://search.ebscohost.com> 2007

(continued)

(continued)

(continued)

Bibliographic Access

- *Magazines for Libraries (Katz)*

- *MedBioWorld <http://www.medbioworld.com>*

- *MediaFinder <http://www.mediafinder.com/>*

- *Ulrich's Periodicals Directory: The Global Source for Periodicals Information Since 1932 <http://www.bowkerlink.com>*

Special Bibliographic Notes related to special journal issues (separates) and indexing/abstracting:

- indexing/abstracting services in this list will also cover material in any "separate" that is co-published simultaneously with Haworth's special thematic journal issue or DocuSerial. Indexing/abstracting usually covers material at the article/chapter level.
- monographic co-editions are intended for either non-subscribers or libraries which intend to purchase a second copy for their circulating collections.
- monographic co-editions are reported to all jobbers/wholesalers/approval plans. The source journal is listed as the "series" to assist the prevention of duplicate purchasing in the same manner utilized for books-in-series.
- to facilitate user/access services all indexing/abstracting services are encouraged to utilize the co-indexing entry note indicated at the bottom of the first page of each article/chapter/contribution.
- this is intended to assist a library user of any reference tool (whether print, electronic, online, or CD-ROM) to locate the monographic version if the library has purchased this version but not a subscription to the source journal.
- individual articles/chapters in any Haworth publication are also available through the Haworth Document Delivery Service (HDDS).

As part of Haworth's continuing committment to better serve our library patrons, we are proud to be working with the following electronic services:

AGGREGATOR SERVICES

EBSCOhost

Ingenta

J-Gate

Minerva

OCLC FirstSearch

Oxmill

SwetsWise

FirstSearch

SwetsWise

LINK RESOLVER SERVICES

1Cate (Openly Informatics)

ChemPort (American Chemical Society)

CrossRef

Gold Rush (Coalliance)

LinkOut (PubMed)

LINKplus (Atypon)

LinkSolver (Ovid)

LinkSource with A-to-Z (EBSCO)

Resource Linker (Ulrich)

SerialsSolutions (ProQuest)

SFX (Ex Libris)

Sirsi Resolver (SirsiDynix)

Tour (TDnet)

Vlink (Extensity, formerly Geac)

WebBridge (Innovative Interfaces)

1cate

ChemPort·

Gold Rush

 LinkOut.

 atypon

 LinkSolver

ULRICH'S RESOURCE LINKER

SerialsSolutions

S·F·X

SirsiDynix

TUR

((extensity))

WebBridge

ABOUT THE EDITORS

James A. Swartz, PhD, is Associate Professor at the University of Illinois at Chicago, in the Jane Addams College of Social Work (JACSW) where he teaches statistics, mental health policy, healthcare in criminal justice settings, and research methods. Dr. Swartz is Principal Investigator on the NIDA-funded Jane Addams Substance Abuse Research Collaborative (JASARC) project to enhance research infrastructure within the College. He is also the PI on a study of the prevalence of co-occurring substance use, psychiatric, and medical conditions and service access among men and women jail detainees. His current research interests are in diagnosis and screening of co-occurring disorders, and on the intersections and common pathways among substance abuse, mental illness, psychopathy, and medical problems. Dr. Swartz has served as co-editor for special issues of *Contemporary Drug Problems*, as a regular reviewer for *Criminal Justice and Behavior*, and as an occasional reviewer for *Archives of General Psychiatry*, the *International Journal of Substance Use and Misuse*, *Crime and Delinquency*, and the *American Journal of Public Health*. He has also served as a proposal reviewer for the Robert Wood Johnson Foundation, and as a special panel reviewer for NIDA.

Patricia O'Brien, PhD, is Associate Professor in the Jane Addams College of Social Work at the University of Illinois at Chicago. Her research, building on ten years of practice, has focused primarily on the description of women's transition from prison as exemplified by her book *Making It in the Free World: Women in Transition from Prison*. She has continued this research, recently completing a three-year longitudinal study funded by NIJ and more recently a NIDA-funded pilot study examining both individual and community factors for released women in an African-American community on Chicago's west side. She has published articles on women's reentry from prison, issues in doing research with women in prison and during the transition to the community, and holistic assessment for women at the time of release to the community.

Arthur J. Lurigio, PhD, is a psychologist, Associate Dean for Faculty in the College of Arts and Sciences, and Professor of Criminal Justice and Psychology at Loyola University Chicago. He is also a member of the Graduate Faculty and Director of the Center for the Advancement of

Research, Training, and Education (CARTE) at Loyola University Chicago, and a Senior Research Advisor at Illinois Treatment Alternatives for Safe Communities (TASC). In 2003, Dr. Lurigio was named a faculty scholar, the highest honor bestowed on senior faculty at Loyola University Chicago. Dr. Lurigio's research is primarily in the areas of offender drug abuse and dependence problems, mental disorders and crime, community corrections, police-community relations, criminal victimization, and victim services. In recognition of the overall outstanding contributions of his research to criminology and criminal justice practices, Dr. Lurigio was conferred the highly prestigious University of Cincinnati Award in 1996 and the Hans W. Mattick Award in 2003.

Drugs, Women, and Justice: Roles of the Criminal Justice System for Drug-Affected Women

CONTENTS

Introduction

James A. Swartz

In September 2005, the Jane Addams College of Social Work sponsored a symposium entitled *Drugs, Women, and Justice: A Research Perspective*. The *Symposium* was part of the activities carried out by the Jane Addams Substance Abuse Research Collaboration (JASARC), a project funded by the National Institute on Drug Abuse (NIDA) to build research infrastructure at the College. The purpose of the *Symposium* was to convene a group of distinguished researchers and research savvy practitioners to present and discuss policy and research issues surrounding the treatment, rehabilitation, and reengagement of drug-involved women under the supervision of the criminal justice system and their families. Two related goals were to develop a research agenda for further study and to broadly disseminate research findings and policy issues addressed at the symposium.

The papers that comprise this volume were originally presented at the *Drugs, Women, and Justice* symposium and reflect the distillation of the latest research and thinking in the complex and still emerging areas of policy and treatment for women in the criminal justice system; many of whom are under supervision specifically because they use and abuse alcohol and other drugs. Although many issues and topics were covered during the three-day *Symposium*, we believe the papers in this volume reflect the diversity and depth of the issues that were covered. (Copies of the slide presentations for some of the papers presented at the

[Haworth co-indexing entry note]: "Introduction." Swartz, James A. Co-published simultaneously in *Women & Criminal Justice* (The Haworth Press, Inc.) Vol. 17, No. 2/3, 2006, pp. 1-4; and: *Drugs, Women, and Justice: Roles of the Criminal Justice System for Drug-Affected Women* (ed: James A. Swartz, Patricia O'Brien, and Arthur J. Lurigio) The Haworth Press, Inc., 2006, pp. 1-4. Single or multiple copies of this article are available for a fee from The Haworth Document Delivery Service [1-800-HAWORTH, 9:00 a.m. - 5:00 p.m. (EST). E-mail address: docdelivery@haworthpress.com].

doi:10.1300/J012v17n02_01

Symposium are available at the JASARC web site: http://www.uic.edu/
jaddams/college/subabuse/present/drugs.html.)

All first authors presented at the *Symposium* and all agreed to transform
their presentations into papers for publication in this volume. The
selected papers touch on a number of critical issues facing those who
work with women in the criminal justice system including: tailoring
interventions to the unique needs of women; the consequences of overly
punitive policies that work against family preservation once a woman is
incarcerated; the service needs and characteristics of the children of
women under the supervision of the criminal justice system; and issues
around community reentry and reintegration following incarceration.

In the first paper, Faye Taxman and her colleague provide a summary
and overview of research on the characteristics of drug-involved women
in the criminal justice system, and the known effectiveness of various
sociological, psychological, and medical interventions designed to address
the multiple and specific service needs of these women. This paper provides context for the others that follow by tracing the contours of recent
research, implicitly showing where there are significant gaps in our understanding of what works best for women and under what circumstances.

The next paper is also an overview, but of policy issues. Patricia Allard
describes how the coupling of harshly punitive drug laws, which result in
lengthy prison sentences for many women, with recently enacted child
welfare legislation works against family reunification even when the
mother may be able to demonstrate that she has been rehabilitated and able
to care for her children. Allard then discusses how the resultant fracturing
of families can be reversed by relying more on diversion programs and
treatment in lieu of incarceration.

Because, in many instances, women in the criminal justice system are
the primary caretakers of their children–as compared with men in the
criminal justice system–the affects of a woman's criminal justice involvement on her children, particularly when she is incarcerated, can be
profound. Accordingly, the paper by Susan Phillips examines the service
needs of children whose mothers have been arrested and criminally
involved at some point in their child's life. Examining the mix of service
needs of children with arrested mothers, she describes a taxonomy for
conceptually and pragmatically assessing and managing the multiple needs
of this heterogeneous population.

Arguably, no one is more affected by the criminalization of drug-
involved women than the women themselves. The next three papers in
the issue deal with the service needs and profiles of women who have
either been in drug treatment, are currently in drug treatment, or are

reentering their communities following incarceration. Elizabeth Essex and her colleagues highlight the central psychological and social importance of loneliness in the lives of criminally involved women who, at times, despite living with their children and other family members, experience a sense of isolation that influences their daily interactions and possibly the course of their rehabilitations. Sheryl Pimlott Kubiak and her colleague examine differences between women in drug treatment and drug-involved women in the criminal justice system who might enter a community-based drug program while under supervision. Their findings that women with criminal justice involvement are demographically different and have more complex service needs argue for further refinements of gender-specific treatment to account for the heterogeneity of women in community-based treatment programs. Patricia O'Brien also examines the specific service needs of women in the criminal justice system, but in the context of release from prison and community resources. She reports on a qualitative study that found women were resilient in the face of many challenges including a paucity of services in the communities to which they returned as well as economic struggles owing to difficulties finding employment. Her work highlights, among other things, the under-appreciated importance of the community context for the rehabilitation and reintegration of women returning home from prison.

The last three papers diverge from the research focus of the previous papers to reflect the balance between policy, treatment, and applied research we sought to achieve at the UIC *Symposium.* Jacqueline Robarge details the developmental history and current service model of a program called *Power Inside* that she and her colleagues developed in Baltimore for women who have survived traumatic violence, working in the street economy, and the criminal justice system. Throughout her paper, she highlights how the program was developed through an ongoing dialog and collaboration with the women who needed services so that the resultant service model was truly responsive to the needs of program participants. Her paper serves as a guide not only for a program model tailored to the specific needs of women but also for how programs can be shaped by including participants in the development process.

Jeremy Travis reminds us, in his paper, that the effects of the current social experiment in "mass incarceration" have both direct and indirect effects on women. He describes the gender imbalance created in communities with high incarceration rates and how the absence of men in these communities–primarily poor and African-American–socially and financially affects women who must bear multiple burdens in their absence. He suggests that research studying issues related to drugs and justice consider this broader class of effects on women, their families, and their social networks not only while men are incarcerated but also when they reenter their communities.

In the final paper, Beth Richie argues for an expanded research perspective that includes the concept of social justice when examining the causes and consequences of women's involvement in the criminal justice system. She notes that while many studies of women in the criminal justice system frame their research questions from the perspective of understanding individual issues, the contribution of contextual factors underlying the social injustices that contribute to the economic marginalization of women and particularly women of color, for instance, have not been well studied or considered as explanatory variables. Her challenge to researchers is to develop theoretical frameworks and measures for assessing how women are harmed by social injustices and how individual-level factors interact with these macro-level factors to create systemic inequities.

Putting this volume together required the work of a number of people whose contributions I would like to briefly acknowledge. First, I would like to thank the editor of *Women & Criminal Justice*, Donna Hale, for graciously agreeing to publish a special issue on this topic and for working with us to make it happen expeditiously. Patricia O'Brien and Arthur Lurigio gave generously of their time and talents to co-edit this volume by reviewing and commenting on all of the papers as well as coordinating the reviews by external reviewers. As we were putting this volume together, external reviewers anonymously provided comments and critiques of the included papers. They may now be named and profusely thanked for their contributions: Bill Barton, Dana Britton, Kathy Farkas, Margaret Severson and Diane Young. And last, thanks to Elisabeth Widmar of the JASARC research staff who brought order and timeliness to the editing process, as well as to Kim Weber who was critical to organizing the original symposium.

Women and the Criminal Justice System: Improving Outcomes Through Criminal Justice and Non-Criminal Justice Responses

Faye S. Taxman
Karen L. Cropsey

SUMMARY. Proportionately women offenders are growing among the ranks of those involved in the correctional system in the U.S. This paper presents an overview of the characteristics of women offenders, our state of knowledge about programs and services for women, and policy choices regarding how to handle the increasing number of women in the criminal justice system. Using the evidence-based practices literature, the needs of the women are compared to the research on effective practices using the Risk-Needs-Responsivity model. This model purports that low risk offenders should not be the priority for intensive services in the criminal justice system; instead high risk offenders should receive such services. Based on this model, the paper discusses whether services in the criminal

Faye S. Taxman, PhD, is Professor and Karen L. Cropsey, PsyD, is Assistant Professor, Virginia Commonwealth University, Wilder School of Government and Public Affairs, 923 West Franklin Street, Richmond, VA 23284-2028.
Address correspondence to: Faye S. Taxman (E-mail: fstaxman@vcu.edu).

The authors would like to acknowledge the assistance of Ms. Jacqueline LaForet-Thiard in the preparation of this paper.

[Haworth co-indexing entry note]: "Women and the Criminal Justice System: Improving Outcomes Through Criminal Justice and Non-Criminal Justice Responses." Taxman, Faye S., and Karen L. Cropsey. Co-published simultaneously in *Women & Criminal Justice* (The Haworth Press, Inc.) Vol. 17, No. 2/3, 2006, pp. 5-26; and: *Drugs, Women, and Justice: Roles of the Criminal Justice System for Drug-Affected Women* (ed: James A. Swartz, Patricia O'Brien, and Arthur J. Lurigio) The Haworth Press, Inc., 2006, pp. 5-26. Single or multiple copies of this article are available for a fee from The Haworth Document Delivery Service [1-800-HAWORTH, 9:00 a.m. - 5:00 p.m. (EST). E-mail address: docdelivery@haworthpress.com].

Available online at http://wcj.haworthpress.com
doi:10.1300/J012v17n02_02

justice system are the best option given the consequences of involving the correctional system to assist women who are poor, underskilled, and undereducated to become productive citizens. doi:10.1300/J012v17n02_02
[Article copies available for a fee from The Haworth Document Delivery Service: 1-800-HAWORTH. E-mail address: <docdelivery@haworthpress.com> Website: <http://www.HaworthPress.com> © *2006 by The Haworth Press, Inc. All rights reserved.]*

KEYWORDS. Women offenders, Risk-Needs-Responsivity model, effective treatment for women, policy alternatives for women offenders

INTRODUCTION

Traditionally, criminology and criminal justice has focused on the study of men, both as the offender and the victim. Theories about offending and punishment have predominantly been based on males, as well as have programs to alter the behavior of offenders. Relatively less attention has been paid towards the role of women in the criminal justice system. Although most inmates incarcerated today are still males, the number of female inmates has grown tremendously in the past decade. Between 1990 and 1999 the number of women in prison rose by 106 percent, whereas the number of men in prison rose 75 percent (Mumola, 2000). In addition, between 1995 and 2003 the number of women on probation rose by 30 percent, which is a slightly higher rate than male probationers (25%; Bureau of Justice Statistics, 1996; Glaze & Palla, 2004). Official government estimates of the correctional population illustrate that the female correctional population is increasing at higher rates than the male population.

Gender-specific studies are needed because the available research indicates that female offenders differ from their male counterparts in several significant ways such as: type of offense(s), socioeconomic status, substance abuse problems, histories of physical or sexual abuse, mental health problems, and their role as a primary caretaker of minor children. A better understanding of these differences is needed to advance our knowledge about effective policies and programs (and/or services) that will reduce recidivism among women offenders, and better provide for women who are victims of criminal acts.

CHARACTERISTICS OF FEMALE OFFENDERS

Type of Offense

When it comes to type of offenses, women are significantly less likely to have committed a violent offense. For women held in jail, only 12 percent are charged with a violent offense. Among those incarcerated in state prison 28 percent are being held for a violent offense whereas 50 percent of males in prison are being held for a violent offense. In federal prison 7 percent of the women are incarcerated for a violent offense (Greenfeld & Snell, 1999; Harrison & Beck, 2003), with most of these incidents of violence against a spouse, ex-spouse, or ex-boyfriend (Covington, 2000). In addition, the types of crimes committed by women are also different from their male counterparts, with the majority of women behind bars due to a property or a minor drug offense. For example, for women in the federal system, 72 percent are incarcerated for a drug offense. For women in local jails, property and drug offenses combined make up 64 percent of the detainees (Greenfeld & Snell, 1999). A recent ethnographic study of women and drug distribution indicated that women occupied the lowest echelons of drug dealing where they assumed the majority of the risk of being caught and prosecuted for a drug-related crime (Maher et al., 1998).

Socioeconomic Status

Like their male counterparts, most female offenders are poor, under-educated, and unskilled. Women offenders, however, tend to have an even lower socioeconomic status than male offenders. A survey taken of jail inmates found that 60 percent of the females were unemployed at the time of the arrest and of those, a third had not been seeking employment. That same study also found that less than a third of the male inmates were unemployed at the time of their arrest (Collins & Collins, 1996). A study conducted by the Department of Justice found that 37 percent of the women in prison who had been working prior to incarceration had an income of $600 or less. Only 28 percent of male prison inmates fell into the same category. Furthermore, nearly 30 percent of female inmates, compared to 8 percent of male inmates, reported receiving welfare assistance prior to their arrest (Greenfeld & Snell, 1999). Most jobs held by many of these women were low-skilled, minimum wage, entry-level jobs. Two-thirds of the women reported never having a job that paid more than $6.50 per hour (Bloom, Owen & Covington, 2003).

A U.S. study found that of those not working at a legitimate job prior to incarceration, 16 percent made money from selling drugs and 15 percent were involved in prostitution, shoplifting, or other illegal activities (Bloom, Chesney-Lind & Owen, 1994).

Substance Abuse

Substance abuse and dependency are problems for women offenders. The rates of using drugs in the month prior to committing their offense is 62 percent for women compared to 56 percent for men. Women were also more likely to have committed their offense while under the influence of drugs, 40 percent compared to 32 percent for men (Mumola, 1999). At local jails, researchers found that 52 percent of female jail inmates were found to be dependent on alcohol or drugs, compared to 44 percent of male inmates (Karberg & James, 2005). These gender differences are the reverse of the substance abuse rates among the general population, where men are twice as likely as women to be dependent on alcohol or drugs (National Survey on Drug Use and Health, 2004). In the general population, these gender differences are believed to be more largely related to a differential in opportunity to use substances and that when similar opportunities to use alcohol or illicit drugs are present for men and women, similar rates of dependency have been shown (Van Etten & Anthony, 1999). When compared to women in the general population it appears that women in jail and prison are six to ten times more likely to have a substance abuse problem (Covington, 2000). In the last data collection for the Arrestee Drug Abuse Monitoring Program conducted in 25 major U.S. cities, on average 35.3 percent of the females tested positive for crack/cocaine, 31.6 percent tested positive for marijuana, 8.8 percent tested positive for methamphetamine, 6.6 percent tested positive for opiates and 86.4 percent tested positive for alcohol (Zhang, 2003). And, half of the women were found to be in need of treatment (Taylor, Fitzgerald, Hung, Reardon & Brownstein, 2003). Overall, female prisoners had almost twice the rates of opioid use in the six months prior to incarceration compared to male prisoners (Brooke et al., 1998). Recent research by Belenko and Peugh (2005), who reanalyzed the Bureau of Justice Statistics 1987 inmate survey, found that half of women offenders were drug dependent and in need of intensive treatment services compared to one-third of the male prisoners.

Research has suggested that women and men differ in their trajectories of substance use and abuse. Females tend to initiate substance use later in life but show a more rapid escalation in substance use including drug dependency. Women initiated alcohol and marijuana use one to two years later than men but progressed to cocaine use one year earlier (Haas et al., 2000). Also, men and women differed in their strategies for obtaining drugs; men were more likely to purchase drugs with cash whereas women were more likely to use non-cash or to trade sex for drugs (Rodriguez & Griffin, 2005), putting themselves at high risk for sexually transmitted diseases and HIV. Accordingly, HIV-infection rates are generally higher among female prisoners in most regions of the United States: Northeast (9.1% females and 4.7% males), Midwest (1.2% females and 1.0% males), South (3.8% females and 2.1% males) and West (0.6% females and 0.8% males). In 2001, 2,145 female prisoners (2.9%) and 19,868 (1.9%) male prisoners were known to be HIV+ (Maruschak, 2004).

Family Background

Along with being impoverished and having substance abuse problems, many of the women in the criminal justice system have histories of an unstable childhood. Six out of ten women in the criminal justice system grew up with only one parent present in the household, usually the mother. Compared to the general population, female inmates are twice as likely to have grown up in a single-parent household (Snell, 1994). Furthermore, approximately 17 percent of women inmates lived in foster care or in a group home at some point during their childhood. Incarcerated women (50%) are also more likely than men (37%) to have at least one family member who has been incarcerated (Bloom et al., 2003). Lastly, a third of female inmates reported having a parent or guardian who abused either alcohol or drugs while the inmate was growing up (Snell, 1994).

Physical and Sexual Abuse

Physical and sexual abuse are more prevalent among the prison population than in the general population (Bloom et al., 2003). Almost half of the female correctional population reported past abuse. Between 23 percent and 37 percent of female offenders reported being either sexually or physically abused before the age of 18. This percentage is much lower among the female general population with numbers ranging between 12 percent and 17 percent. Female inmates growing up in foster care or other institutions reported being abused at an alarmingly high rate of 86.7 percent. Of those inmates growing up with at least one parent, 75.7 percent reported that their parent abused alcohol or drugs. Female inmates who were abused as an adult overwhelmingly reported being abused by a spouse or boyfriend. In State prison, 25 percent of the women reported being abused both as a juvenile and an adult. Substance abuse by women highly correlates with a history of physical and sexual abuse. Among abused women in state prison, 89 percent reported using illegal drugs regularly whereas female inmates without histories of abuse reported regular drug use at 65 percent (Harlow, 1999).

Mothers/Caretakers

An important difference between men and women offenders is that women offenders are usually primary caretakers of minor children prior to their incarceration. The majority (70%) of the female correctional population are mothers of at least one minor child. It is estimated that approximately 1.3 million children have a mother under correctional supervision and at least 250,000 children under the age of 18 have a mother who is in jail or prison (Bloom, Owen & Covington, 2003). Prior to admission 64.3 percent of women state prison inmates, reported living with their children. The mean age of the children left behind is 8 years old, with 22 percent of incarcerated mothers reporting a child under 5 years old in the home. In contrast to male inmates who reported that the mother of their child was the primary caregiver of their children (90%), only 28 percent of incarcerated mothers reported that the father of their children was the primary caregiver. The majority of incarcerated mothers reported that their children were being taken care of by grandparents (53%), other relatives (26%), or in foster care (10%). Visitation with their children while incarcerated was infrequent with only 24 percent of female state prison inmates reporting that they had visited with their children since admission (Mumola, 2000).

Mental Health

Female detainees have mental illnesses at a higher rate than their male counterparts. Approximately 24 percent of female prison and jail inmates report a mental illness. Among female probationers, 22 percent are identified as mentally ill compared to about 15 percent of male inmates and probationers who reported a mental illness (Ditton, 1999). Depression was the most common psychiatric disorder followed by bipolar disorder and post-traumatic stress disorder (PTSD; Hills, 2002). Rates of PTSD are particularly high among female correctional populations. A recent study found that among female jail inmates waiting to stand trial, 33.5 percent were suffering from PTSD (Zlotnick, 2002).

INTERVENTIONS USED WITH FEMALE OFFENDERS

Since women in prison (and probation) appear to be quite different from their male counterparts in many significant ways, it would make sense that interventions provided to these women would also need to be tailored to their individuals needs. However, correctional research involving interventions with women have largely been ignored, likely due to the fact that the incarceration of women was traditionally viewed as an anomaly. And, while it was required for federal grants to include women in the studies, the studies do not tend to examine issues specific to female populations, instead applying the male-based treatments to the female population. However, Chesney-Lind (1998; 2000) argued that with the advent of the women's movement and demands for equality, the courts have responded by giving women harsh sentences, "equality with a vengeance." Thus in recent years, with changes in mandatory minimum sentencing and "three-strikes" laws, women have become further enmeshed in a legal system that was designed to accommodate the male (more serious) offender and was not designed for the non-violent property or drug offender, which is the bulk of female crime.

Similarly, correctional treatment and programs have been designed for men and applied haphazardly to women with the expectation of similar results (Covington, 1998). The majority of the interventions that have been tested with women are minor modifications of a similar male intervention, even though in 1994 the Center for Substance Abuse Treatment (CSAT) developed a list of issues that should be incorporated into any comprehensive treatment program for women. Similarly, Covington (1998) noted that four main themes emerged from interviewing women in recovery: sense of self, relationships, sexuality, and spirituality. A brief review of the major types of interventions that have been tested specifically with female offenders will be reviewed.

Rehabilitation and Recidivism

A meta-analysis by Dowden and Andrews (1999) investigated the question of what works for female offenders in terms of preventing recidivism. Using the Risk, Need, and Responsivity (RNR) framework (Andrews & Bonta, 1998; Andrews, Bonta et al., 1990) for determining recidivism. Dowden and Andrews (1999) examined 26 independent studies of female offenders. The RNR framework provides that actuarial risk should guide the provision of services with a focus on interventions that address the criminogenic needs of offenders that are most directly linked to recidivism such as substance dependency, peer associations and networks, low self-control, anti-social value systems, criminal personality, and family dysfunctions (Andrews, Bonta, & Wormith, 2006). They noted that the strongest predictors of treatment success were interventions that targeted interpersonal criminogenic needs (e.g., family and peer associations, etc.) generally, and family process variables, in particular. Interventions that targeted personal and interpersonal non-criminogenic needs (e.g., mental health status, low self-esteem, etc.) were not associated with positive outcomes, and in fact, these targets appeared to increase recidivism within the intervention groups (Dowden & Andrews, 1999). Generally such programs did not address the criminogenic needs that contributed to the women's involvement in criminal behavior. Other behavioral targets such as substance abuse and education skills that were previously believed to be important by correctional administrators were not found to be significantly related in this meta-analysis. This study found that interventions that have been shown to be effective for male offenders in reducing recidivism appeared to also be effective for female offenders (Dowden & Andrews, 1999). However, given that they used the RNR framework, which illustrates that interventions are more likely to be effective for higher risk offenders (and women tend to not score in this category given the nature of their offenses), it is likely that the meta-analysis could not identify effective gender specific interventions for women. Many of the women in the studies would have scored lower risk than their male counterparts. Women overall do not benefit from correctional interventions because they tend to be low risk and less likely to recidivate overall. Thus, the few studies that have been conducted with women offenders do not differentiate between women who are high risk for reoffending and lower risk women, which may explain why the meta-analysis did not reveal any specific interventions that are more effective for women or men.

Substance Abuse

Few studies of substance abuse treatment applied specifically to treatment of women in the criminal justice system have been presented in the literature. A meta-analysis examining the effectiveness of women's substance abuse treatment programs (Orwin, Francisco & Bernichon, 2001) noted an overall positive effect in most domains of substance abuse treatment. In particular, Orwin and colleagues made three group comparisons: (1) women who received treatment compared to women who received no treatment, (2) women in women-only treatment programs compared to women in mixed gender treatment programs, and (3) women who received standard substance abuse treatment services compared to women who received enhanced substance abuse treatment services. For each of those groups, they compared women on the following outcome domains (when possible): alcohol use, drug use, psychiatric problems, psychological well-being, attitudes/ beliefs, HIV risk behavior, criminal activity, and pregnancy outcomes (Orwin et al., 2001).

Women who received treatment versus women who did not receive substance abuse treatment were assessed on six domains with the finding that five of the six outcomes were positive while the sixth was essentially zero. (Note that effect sizes is a standard method of describing impact of the intervention with small referring to 0-.20 and medium .21 to .40.) Three of the effect sizes are considered small: alcohol use (0.13), drug use (0.17), and criminal activity (0.16)] while two effect sizes were medium [psychiatric problems (0.41) and pregnancy outcomes 0.33)]. Women in gender-specific groups versus mixed groups also demonstrated small to medium positive effects over six domains. In five domains the effects were small [alcohol use (0.15), other drug use (0.04), psychological well-being (0.06), and criminal activity (0.16)] while a medium positive effect was seen for psychiatric problems (0.30). Finally, when comparing enhanced versus standard substance abuse treatment, women who received the enhanced substance abuse treatment demonstrated a large positive effect in the domains of psychological well-being (0.57), attitudes and beliefs (0.61) and pregnancy outcomes (0.64). A medium positive effect was seen for HIV risk behavior (0.33), while psychiatric problems and drug use both demonstrated a small positive effect (0.18 and 0.14, respectively). No effect was demonstrated for alcohol use or criminal activities from enhanced substance abuse services (Orwin et al., 2001). Overall, the results from this meta-analysis demonstrate that interventions with female substance abusers are generally effective across a variety of domains.

Several new pharmacotherapeutic agents have recently received FDA-approval for use in the United States. These newer treatments include buprenorphine/naloxone (Suboxone®) for opiate addiction and acamprosate (Campral®) and depot naltrexone (Vivatrol®) for alcohol dependence. Despite these new treatments, a recent review article of pharmacotherapies for substance abuse treatment among offenders noted a dearth of research in this area for both male and female offenders (Cropsey, Villalobos, & St. Clair, 2005). Further, the majority of the studies have been conducted with male inmates exclusively, while the studies that contained both male and female offenders did not offer any gender comparisons.

HIV Prevention

While there has been a recent explosion of articles in the HIV-prevention literature calling for prevention strategies for incarcerated individuals (see Spaulding et al., 2002), few intervention studies have been reported. Early studies of HIV-prevention for incarcerated women focused on providing information and enhancing HIV risk-reduction skills, with mixed results. Magura, Kang, Shapiro & O'Day (1995) found no difference in drug use or sexual risk behavior after an AIDS-education program for drug-using women in jail. However, women who entered prison with a recent history of substance abuse showed enhanced safer sex behavior, coping skills and perceived emotional support after a 16-session in-prison HIV-prevention intervention (El-Bassel et al., 1995). Martin, O'Connell, Inciardi, Surrat & Beard (2003) compared an enhanced version of the NIDA standard HIV intervention to a Focused Intervention based on a cognitive-behavioral thought-mapping model and noted that while there were no differences between two HIV-prevention interventions at the six month follow-up, significant reductions in substance use and unprotected sex were seen between baseline and follow-up. A comparison of two theory-based interventions for incarcerated women showed increases in risk reduction skills for women in the intervention based on social cognitive theory and greater commitment to change among women in the intervention based on a theory of gender and power (St. Lawrence et al., 1997). Similarly, an individual and group counseling intervention with incarcerated women showed that inmates changed their attitudes, self-efficacy and intentions to change HIV-risk behavior (Bauserman et al., 2003).

However, changes in attitudes toward HIV-prevention during incarceration are not necessarily reflected in changes in risk behavior after release. A comparison of a sexual risk reduction intervention with a drug relapse intervention showed that, while women improved in knowledge and attitudes toward HIV-prevention in prison, these were not followed by differential changes in risk behavior after release. The researchers speculated that the lack of transfer from prison to "free world" might have been due to the magnitude of other problems faced by women leaving prison and the relatively lower priority of HIV-risk reduction (Eldridge & St. Lawrence, 2001; Eldridge et al., 2000). More recently, interventions have begun to focus on HIV-risk reduction in the context of Transitional Case Management, addressing reentry issues simultaneously with HIV-risk reduction (Motta-Moss, Freudenberg, Young, Gallagher, 2000; Richie, Freudenberg, & Page, 2001; Vigilante et al., 1999). However,

TCM for reducing HIV risk has been applied to male inmates and has not been widely implemented or investigated with women.

Trauma

A recent review article examining trauma interventions with prisoner populations noted a tremendous need for further study in this area (Heckman, Cropsey, & Olds-Davis, in press). In particular, they noted that only eight empirical studies have investigated this issue and many of these studies were methodologically flawed by having weak designs, small samples, and inadequate follow-up or outcome measures (Heckman et al., in press). Specifically, they noted only four studies of interventions with women with trauma. Two studies (Colisetti & Thyer, 2000; Valentine & Smith, 2001) used an exposure therapy approach while the other two studies used a skills based intervention (Zlotnick, Najavits, Rohsenow & Johnson, 2003; Salerno, 2005). Only two interventions (Zlotnick et al., 2003; Valentine & Smith, 2001) reported reductions in PTSD symptoms (Heckman et al., in press). No studies investigating pharmacotherapy approaches for PTSD (used either alone or in conjunction with cognitive and behavioral interventions) have been reported in the literature with this population despite the demonstrated efficacy of pharmacotherapies, particularly Selective Serotonin Reuptake Inhibitors (SSRIs), for alleviating PTSD symptoms (Putnam & Hulsmann, 2002).

FUTURE DIRECTIONS

The growing percentage of women involved in corrections–from probation to prison–implies that the criminal justice net is being cast more widely. The "war on drugs" has contributed to individuals being arrested repeatedly. Even if an offender's record consists of mostly minor offenses, the longer the criminal record, the more likely the offender will receive a more restrictive sentence (jail and prison). This has been the sentencing pattern developed over the last 30 years, mostly in response to the belief that wrongdoers should be punished based on the nature of the offense and the severity (length) of the criminal record. "Three strikes and you're out" sentencing philosophies advance the tendency to use incarceration, even if the offenses are minor. The general sentencing philosophy is that offenders who continue to commit their crimes should be punished more punitively, even for minor crimes or victimless crimes (e.g., prostitution, etc.). It is not surprising that today women are the fastest growing segment of the correctional population given our history with punishment (and rehabilitation). The question before us is how capable is the criminal justice system in addressing the needs of women offenders, particularly if we are interested in desistance from criminal behavior and not merely punishment.

Recent research on desistance is that it is most likely to occur from social bonds that reinforce positive behavior, interventions that assist individuals in becoming prosocial, and maturation or pathways that reinforce ascribed roles of providers (e.g., work, marriage, wage-earner, etc.). Yet, as this review has illustrated, it has become clear that women are different from men, especially in terms of the nature of social bonds, a women's role in society, and the types of intervention that are likely to yield better outcomes. The pathways that lead women to crime are inherently different then those of their male counterparts. To assist women in becoming more productive citizens, the interventions and/services should be geared to addressing the criminogenic risk and need factors specific to women. The tools that the criminal justice system uses to assess risk and criminogenic needs factors might also need to be altered too, to reflect the different dimensions that are more applicable to women (e.g., for men, the family issues may be related to need to be a breadwinner whereas for women it might be the demands of being a caretaker; dysfunctional relationships for women may be related to their relationship with and the influence of men in their lives as compared to gangs or companions for men, etc.). Stated simply, women are different than men in a number of dimensions and yet criminological, substance abuse, mental health, and other related areas of research have failed to assist practitioners to translate these differences into programs and services that are designed to reduce the risk of recidivism among women offenders. And, the translation to policy has yet to occur.

OVERVIEW OF CRIMINOGENIC NEEDS
THAT AFFECT (RECIDIVISM) OUTCOMES

Lack of Healthy Relationships

Women offenders are likely to have a lack of a healthy, stable relationship(s). Disconnection and abuse characterize the history of many female offenders. A study conducted of women at a Massachusetts prison found that 38 percent had lost a parent during childhood, 69 percent had histories of abuse and 70 percent had left home before the age of seventeen (Covington, 1998). Many of these women participated in prostitution. They reported being with men that beat them, men that robbed them, men that used them, and men that did not take care of their children. Many women also attribute their drug usage to their previous partners since females are often first introduced to drugs by their partner. These women then continue to take drugs believing it necessary in order to stay with their partner and often times their partners continue to supply the drugs for them (Covington, 2002). In such cases women have not experienced a relationship that did not involve the abuse of drugs or alcohol. In addition, since women tend to measure their self-worth through connections with others, women are much more dependent on others compared to males. These factors are important to consider in developing appropriate interventions/services for women, including providing services to assist women who suffer from depression and isolation due to their histories of unsuccessful relationships and their inability to form meaningful connections with other people (Bloom et al., 2005).

Influences on Criminal Conduct

From childhood, females are socialized differently from men. A female's identity is structured around relationships, interdependence and connectedness; whereas, a male's identity is structured around independence and autonomy (Whitaker, 2000). These differences are exhibited in not only the motive for criminal behavior but also the types of crimes males and females are most likely to commit. It is not uncommon for females to commit crimes in order to gain the acceptance of a partner, or as an expression of pain from a history of abuse. Women also engage in crime in order to provide a better way of life for their families (Covington, 2000). For the few females who engage in violent criminal acts, most commit their acts against an intimate partner or relative (Conly, 1998) which makes them lower risk to commit future offenses but their crime is of such seriousness that it warrants severe punishment.

Substance Abuse and Medical Needs

Female offenders are more likely to have used drugs in the month prior to their incarceration. They were also more likely to have committed crimes in order to gain money for drugs (Conly, 1998; Taylor, et al., 2001). Many reported using drugs not because of the excitement, but to suppress serious emotional pain (Covington, 2000). As previously reported, women are more likely to be dependent on drugs or alcohol, and in need of treatment.

Women offenders tend to have more unique medical needs that require more immediate care than their male counterparts. In 1991, 6 percent of female offenders who entered prison were pregnant (Conly, 1998) and 2.9 percent of females in state prison had AIDS or were HIV positive (compared to 1.9% of male inmates) (Maruschak, 2004). Women inmates entering prison were three times more likely then men to report a history of physical or sexual abuse (Conly, 1998).

Role as Caretakers and Mothers

While the perception is that women who end up incarcerated (or in the criminal justice system) are inadequate and incompetent to care for their children, many mothers feel terribly guilty for being away from their children. One of the most damaging aspects of prison for women is being away from their children (Covington, 2002). A study conducted by the Bureau of Justice in 1997 found that only 23.8 percent of incarcerated females reported having visits with their children, 53.6 percent had phone contact, 65.8 percent had mail contact, and 21.6 percent had no contact at all with their children (Mumola, 2000). Contact with their children plays an important role in morale and recovery. Often, children provide the hope and motivation for women offenders to address their substance abuse and other issues. These important social bonds can be instrumental in helping a women address her behavior.

BUILDING POLICIES, PROGRAMS OR SERVICES TO ADDRESS CRIMINOGENIC NEEDS

According to the RNR model, the above criminogenic needs can be used as factors to both motivate offenders to become interested in improving themselves (and becoming prosocial) and to include in interventions to address factors that propel women into criminal behaviors. A successful intervention program should therefore address all issues related to family violence, drug abuse, unhealthy relationships, and victimization (if it exists; Bloom et al., 2005; Covington, 1998). The road to incarceration for many women begins in childhood where early victimization leads to running away from home. Alone on the streets, prostitution, robbery or selling drugs are often pursued as a means to survival. The abuse of drugs and alcohol are also linked to blunting the pain from these actions, and research demonstrates a strong link between a history of abuse and drug addiction (Bloom & McDiarmid, 2000). Survivors of abuse often exhibit post traumatic stress syndrome, which suggests the need to offer such services to women.

Interventions for women should focus on cognitive and behavioral skill-building where the women can advance themselves. Although such interventions have not been adequately tested on women offenders and/or addicts, they do show promise, particularly those interventions that tend to focus on practical, lifestyle skills that improve one's decision-making and behavioral responses. As recently highlighted by a meta-analysis of cognitive and behavioral programs conducted by Landenberger and Lipsey (2006), the factors associated with recidivism reduction involved CBT programs that included anger control and interpersonal problem solving along with high quality implementation. Programs that included a relatively high degree of role-playing and situational analyses tended to yield better outcomes. For women, it appears that the effective interventions would follow accordingly by providing women with a better understanding of how to maintain and sustain healthy relationships, negotiate their independence and self-sustaining nature, and handle difficult life situations. A consensus in the field is that interventions are best done in the context of a homogenous treatment group where women can be encouraged to engage in safe healing and to allow them to develop good relationships with other members of the group. Tailoring the group to be considerate of the racial, ethnic and cultural differences among the women is also advised (Covington, 2000).

The plight of most women offenders–being poor, undereducated, and disproportionately women of color–suggest that efforts that focus on the women's socioeconomic status would also assist in desistence from crime. While many women lived below the poverty line and required governmental assistance in order to support their families prior to incarceration, this pattern is likely to continue after or during involvement with the criminal justice system. Most women offenders were single parent heads of their households, supporting themselves and children before incarceration. Once released, women are presented with economic demands that often lead them back into a lifestyle of abusing substances and re-offending. Providing education, vocational training and employment services as enhancements to skill building provides a more proactive strategy for providing women with the employability skills to be successful without a life of crime (Bloom et al., 2005).

Reunification with children and/or other family members would also serve to sustain the impact of interventions for women. For many women their primary concern is being reunited with their children. Navigating all the requirements to get their children back is a grueling and complex process that will likely require these women receive help to meet all the conditions (Conly, 1998). If the process of getting her children back becomes too frustrating or hopeless, women offenders may be likely to relapse into substance abuse or other negative behaviors. A good strategy is to prepare a plan for re-entry shortly before release that involves community-based programs. (Another best practice is for community-based programs to enter correctional facilities and help women prepare for release.) For women who do not have a place of residence, this plan should address some of the requirements of safe housing, which will facilitate the women being able to care for her children.

And, lastly, a key factor to successful outcomes is a correctional environment that is safe and where an individual can be comfortable that they will be secure. The correctional environment, particularly for those that are interested in achieving behavior change, must provide a milieu where women (and men) do not feel victimized or do not resort to perpetrator-type of behaviors to protect oneself. Without safety, many women offenders who have histories of physical or sexual abuse may be (re)traumatized. Custodial misconduct that may occur in women's prisons such as rape, sexual harassment, threatening force, and denying goods and privileges (Covington, 2002; Beck & Hughes, 2005) and inmate-to-inmate misconduct can contribute to unsafe environments where women can not be expected to become contributing members of society. Either staff or inmate misbehavior leads to a hostile atmosphere in which female inmates may assume a defensive role. As previously discussed, women thrive in an environment in which they can create trusting relationships, and to learn how to create healthy relationships this can only occur in a healthy environment. The correctional system should provide an environment that allows women to be free from threatening behavior. While little research is available about the type of staffing that is best suited to handle female offenders, an argument can be made that it is preferable to have women officers deal with women offenders (therefore reducing any tensions). It can also be argued that the presence of men can assist women in learning to handle situations outside of the prison walls. The existence of males within female facilities may add tension and undue stress upon the female inmates, unless the environment is such that misconduct by staff (males and/or females) is not tolerated.

CONCLUSION

A major theoretical approach in criminology is Risk-Needs-Responsivity (RNR), which provides a scientific approach to policies and programs (or services) to ameliorate risk factors. This theory suggests that the criminal justice system should provide services and interventions to offenders who are more likely to reoffend (high risk), and to ensure that such interventions respond to the factors that directly affect involvement in criminal behavior. As discussed above, the six factors include antisocial values, criminal peers, dysfunctional families, substance abuse, criminal personality, and low self control. A number of common factors that are secondary issues (e.g., mental health conditions, educational attainment, etc.) might be included to improve the offender's social adjustment or well-being (which may or may not be tied to involvement in criminal behavior). The services/interventions then must be responsive to the criminological needs of women offenders, and recognize the differences between the genders. And women offenders need skill-building services that assist them to engage in healthy relationships, to address substance abuse and deviate peers, and to establish self-sufficiency. Using cognitive-behavioral therapies is most likely to yield more effective interventions for women offenders.

Under RNR theory, high risk offenders should be offered more services under the criminal justice umbrella since good quality (cognitive or cognitive behavioral) services are likely to improve offender outcomes. Since many women do not fit the high risk profile (e.g., history of serious offenses and prior incarcerations), the question is how to address the needs of women offenders. The limited research in this area suggests that the criminal justice net is attracting women who are lower in socioeconomic status and who are not self-sufficient (and they do not have the skills to be self-sufficient). Using incarceration for this subpopulation appears to only further perpetuate a cycle of involvement with the criminal justice system for the greater parts of their life. The consequences of this action is that these women are also mothers and caregivers for their families, and their families will be affected by these decisions. The further involvement of these women in the criminal justice, based on current research, suggests that their children are likely to follow a similar path.

The questions before us are how to address the social ills that propel an increasing number of women into the criminal justice system and whether we have the collective will to assist poor, uneducated, low skilled women, who often have had difficult childhoods, to become productive members of society. Given the current state of the social services in the U.S., women offenders are unlikely to be offered services to advance their lot in society unless the service is provided through the criminal justice or child welfare systems. Although the tendency of many may be to increase programming through the criminal justice system, this is an avenue that should be pursued with a fair degree of caution. The history of the criminal justice system over the last three decades where the "war on drugs" capitalized on criminalization as a means to address anti-social behavior such as substance abuse suggests that expanding the net does not necessarily achieve the desired outcomes of reducing substance abuse or deterring offenders from involvement in criminal conduct. Expanding the net has actually resulting in churning offenders through a process of recidivism and reincarceration, leading the U.S. to have the largest per capita incarceration rate in the world. In many states, corrections systems budgets have grown significantly and are now larger than their primary education budgets.

Using legal coercion may appear to be a useful policy, but as previously suggested, it has a number of collateral consequences that suggest other avenues may be worth pursuing. Moreover, we have tested these collateral consequences on males where it is increasingly recognized that incarceration has not achieved the intended social control goals. Why would we desire to pursue the same path with women (and children)?

REFERENCES

Andrews, D. A., & Bonta, J. (1996). *The psychology of criminal conduct*. Cincinnati, OH: Anderson.

Andrews, D. A. and J. Bonta. (1998). *The Psychology of Criminal Conduc* (2nd ed.). Cincinnati, OH: Anderson Publishing Co.

Andrews, D. A., Bonta, J., and Wormith, J. S. (2006). The Recent Past and Near Future of Risk and/or Need Assessment. *Crime Delinquency, 52*(1): 7-27.

Bauserman, R. L., Richardson, D., Ward, M., Shea, M., Bowlin, C., Tomoyasu, N. et al., (2003). HIV prevention with jail and prison inmates: Maryland's prevention case management program. *AIDS Education and Prevention, 15*, 465-480.

Beck, A. J. & Hughes, T. A. (2005). Sexual Violence Reported by Correctional Authorities, 2004. Bureau of Justice Statistics, NCJ 210333, 1-39.

Belenko, S. & Peugh, J. (2005). *Estimating drug treatment needs among state prison inmates. Drug & Alcohol Dependence, 77*(3), 269-281.

Bloom, B., Chesney-Lind, M., & Owen, B. (1994). Women in California prisons: Hidden victims of the war on drugs. San Francisco: Center on Juvenile and Criminal Justice.

Bloom, B., & Covington, S. (1998). *Gender-specific programming for female offenders: What is it and why is it important?* Paper presented at the 50th Annual Meeting of the American Society of Criminology, Washington, DC.

Bloom, B., Owen, B., & Covington, S. (2003). *Gender-responsive strategies: Research, practice, and guiding principles for women offenders.* Washington, DC: U.S. Department of Justice, National Institute of Corrections.

Bloom, B., Owen, B., & Covington, S. (2005). *Gender-responsive strategies: A summary of tesearch, practice, and guidingprinciples for women offenders.* Washington, DC: U.S. Department of Justice, National Institute of Corrections.

Bloom, B., & McDiarmid, A. (2000). Gender-Responsive Supervision and Programming for Women Offenders in the Community. In National Institute of Corrections. *Topics in community corrections, annual issue 2000: Responding to women offenders in the community.* Washington, DC: National Institute of Corrections.

Brooke, D., Taylor, C., Gunn, J., Maden, A. (1998). Substance misusers remanded to prison a treatment opportunity. *Addiction, 93,* 1851-1856.

Bureau of Justice Statistics. (1996). Washington, DC: U.S. Department of Justice, Bureau of Statistics.

Chesney-Lind, M. (1998). Women in prison: From partial justice to vengeful equity, *Corrections Today, December,* 67-73.

Chesney-Lind, M. (2000). Women and the criminal justice system: Gender matters. *Topics in Community Corrections: Annual Issue, 7-10.* U.S. Department of Justice, National Institute of Correctons.

Colisetti, S.D., & Thyer, B.A. (2000). The relative effectiveness of EMDR versus relaxation training with battered women prisoners. *Behavior Modification, 24,* 719-39.

Collins, W. C., & Collins, A. W. (1996). *Women in jail: Legal issues.* Washington, DC: U.S. Department of Justice, National Institute of Corrections.

Conly, C. (1998). *The Women's Prison Association: Supporting women offenders and their Families.* Washington, DC: U.S. Department of Justice, National Institute of Justice.

Covington, S. (1998). The relational theory of women's psychological development: Implications for the criminal justice system. In Ruth T. Zaplin (Ed.), *Female offenders: Critical perspectives and effective interventions* (pp. 113-131). Gaithersburg, MD: Aspen Publishers.

Covington, S. S. (1998). Women in prison: approaches in the treatment of our most invisible population. *Women in Therapy, 21,* 141-155.

Covington, S. (2000). Helping women to recover: Creating gender-specific treatment for substance-abusing women and girls in community correctional settings. In M. McMahon (Ed.). *Assessment to Assistance: Programs for Women in Community Corrections,* 171-233.

Covington, S. (2002). *A woman's journey home: Challenges for female offenders.* Washington, DC: Urban Institute.

Cropsey, K. L., Villalobos, G. C, & St. Clair, C. (2000). Pharmacotherapy Treatment in Substance-Dependent Correctional Populations: A Review. *Substance Use & Misuse, 40,* 1983-1999.

Ditton, P. M. (1999). *Mental health and treatment of inmates and probationers.* Washington, DC: U.S. Department of Justice, Bureau of Statistics.

Dowden, C. & Andrews, D. A. (1999). What Works for Female Offenders: A Meta-Analytic Review. *Crime & Delinquency, 45*(4), 438-452.

El-Bassel, M., Ivanov, A., Schilling, R. F., Gilbert, L., Borne, D., & Chen, D.-R. (1995). Preventing HIV/AIDS in drug-abusing incarcerated women through skills building and social support enhancement: Preliminary outcomes. *Social Work Research, 19*, 131-141.

Eldridge, G., & St. Lawrence, J. (2001, March). Bridging the gap: HIV-prevention for women in prison. In Cropsey, K. (Chair), *Breaking in: Bringing behavioral medicine into correctional systems.* Symposium conducted at 22nd annual meeting of the Society for Behavioral Medicine, Seattle, WA.

Eldridge, G, St. Lawrence, J., Little, C., Mustafa, V., Shelby, M., & Bockwitz, L. (2000, May). Project WIN: HIV-prevention for women in corrections. In R. Wolitski (Chair), *Bringing it all together to address the needs of incarcerated population.* Symposium conducted at the Drug Use, HIV, and Hepatitis Conference: Bringing it all Together, Baltimore, MD.

Glaze, L., & Palla, S. (2004). *Probation and parole in the United States, 2003.* Washington, DC: U.S. Department of Justice, Bureau of Statistics.

Greenfeld, L. A. & Snell, T. L. (1999). *Women Offenders.* Washington, DC: U.S. Department of Justice, Bureau of Statistics.

Haas, A. L. & Peters, R. H. (2000). Development of substance abuse problems among drug-involved offenders: Evidence for the telescoping effect, *Journal of Substance Abuse, 12*, 241-253.

Harlow, C. (1999). *Prior abuse reported by inmates and probationers.* Washington, DC: U.S. Department of Justice, Bureau of Statistics.

Harrison, P. M., & Beck, A. J. (2003). *Prisoners in 2002.* Washington, DC: U.S. Department of Justice, Bureau of Statistics.

Heckman, C. J., Cropsey, K. L., & Olds-Davis, T. (in press). PTSD treatment in correctional settings: A brief review of the empirical literature. *Psychotherapy.*

Hills, H. (2002). *Treating women with co-occurring disorders involved in the justice system and their children.* Washington, DC: U.S. Department of Health and Human Services, The National GAINS Center.

Karberg, J. & James, J. (2005). *Substance dependence, abuse, and treatment of jail inmates, 2002.* Washington, DC: U.S. Department of Justice, Bureau of Statistics.

Landenberg, N. & Lipsey, M (2005). The postive effects of cognitive-behavioral programs for offenders: A meta anlaysis of factors assocaited with effective treatment. *Journal of Experimental Criminology, 1*, 451-476.

Maher L., Dixon D, Hall W, Lynskey M. (1998). *Running the risks: Heroin, health and harm in South West Sydney.* Sydney: National Drug and Alcohol Research Centre. NDARC Monograph No. 38.

Magura, S., Kang, S.-Y., Shapiro, J. L., & O'Day, J. (1995). Evaluation of an AIDS education model for women drug users in jail. *International Journal of the Addictions, 30*, 259-273.

Martin, S. S., O'Connell, D. J., Inciardi, J. A., Surrat, H. L., & Beard, R. A. (2003). HIV/AIDS among probationers: An assessment of risk and results from a brief intervention. *Journal of Psychoactive Drugs, 35*, 435-443.

Maruschak, L. M. (2004). *HIV in prisons and jails, 2002.* Washington, DC: U.S. Department of Justice, Bureau of Statistics.

Motta-Moss, A., Freudenberg, N., Young, W., & Gallagher, T. (2000). The Fortune Society's Latino discharge planning: A model of comprehensive care for HIV-positive ex-offenders. *Drugs & Society, 16,* 123-144.

Mumola, C. J. (1999). *Substance abuse and treatment, state and federal prisoners, 1997.* Washington, DC: U.S. Department of Justice, Bureau of Statistics.

Mumola, C. J. (2000). *Incarcerated parents and their children.* Washington, DC: U.S. Department of Justice, Bureau of Statistics.

Office of Applied Studies (2004). Results from the 2003 National Survey on Drug Use and Health: National Findings (DHHDS Publication No. SMA 04-3964, HSDUH Series H-25). Rockville, MD: Substance Abuse and Mental Health Services Administration.

Orwin, R. G., Fancisco, L., & Bernichon, T. (2001). Effectiveness of women's substance abuse treatment programs: a meta-analysis. National Evaluation Data Services, Center for Substance Abuse Treatment, Department of Health and Human Services.

Putnam, F. W., & Hulsmann, J. E. (2002). Pharmacotherapy for survivors of childhood trauma, *Seminars in Clinical Neuropsychiatry, 7,* 129-136.

Richie, B. E., Freudenberg, N., & Page, J. (2001). Reintegrating women leaving jail into urban communities: A description of a model program. *Journal of Urban Health, 78,* 290-303.

Rodriguez, N., & Griffin, M. L. (2005). Gender differences in drug market activities: a comparative analysis of men and women's participation in the drug market. U.S. Department of Justice (211974).

Salerno, N. (2005). *The Use of Hypnosis in the Treatment of Post-traumatic Stress Disorder in a Female Correctional Setting. Australian Journal of Clinical & Experimental Hypnosis, 33*(1), 74-81.

Snell, T. L. (1994). *Women in prison: Survey of state prison inmates, 1991.* Washington, DC: U.S. Department of Justice, Bureau of Statistics.

Spaulding, A., Stephenson, B., Macalino, G., Ruby, W., Clarke, J. G., & Flanigan, T. P. (2002). Human immunodeficiency virus in correctional facilities. A review. *Clinical Infectious Diseases, 35,* 305-312.

St. Lawrence, J. S., Eldridge, G. D., Shelby, M. C., Little, C. E., Brasfield, T. L., & O'Bannon, R.E. III (1997). HIV risk reduction for incarcerated women: A comparison of brief interventions based on two theoretical models. *Journal of Consulting and Clinical Psychology, 65,* 504-509.

Taylor, B. G., Fitzgerald, N, Hunt, D., Reardon, J. A., & Brownstein, H. H. (2001). *ADAM preliminary 2000. Findings on drug use and drug markets–adult male arrestees.* Washington DC, Office of Justice Programs, NCJ 189101.

Valentine, P. V., & Smith, T. (2001). Evaluating traumatic incident reduction therapy with female inmates: A randomized controlled clinical trial. *Research on Social Work Practice, 11,* 40-52.

Van Etten, M. L., Anthony, J. C. (1999). Comparative epidemiology of initial drug opportunities and transitions to first use: marijuana, cocaine, hallucinogens and heroin. *Drug and Alcohol Dependence, 54,* 117-125.

Vigilante, K. C., Flynn, M. M., Affleck, P. C., Merriman, N. A., Flanigan, T. P., Mitty, J. A., Rich, J. D. (1999). Reduction in recidivism of incarcerated women through primary care, peer counseling, and discharge planning. *Journal of Women's Health, 8,* 409-415.

Whitaker, M. S. (2000). Equitable does not mean identical. In *Responding to Women Offenders in the Community.* Washington, DC: U.S. Department of Justice, National Institute of Corrections.

Zhang, Z. (2003). *Drug and alcohol use and related matters among arrestees 2003.* Washington, DC: U.S. Department of Justice, Arrestee Drug Abuse Monitoring Program.

Zlotnick, C. (2002). *Treatment of Incarcerated Women With Substance Abuse and Posttraumatic Stress Disorder, Final Report.* Washington, DC: U.S. Department of Justice, National Criminal Reference Service.

Zlotnick, C., Najavits, L., Rohsenow, D. & Johnson, D. (2003). A cognitive-behavioral treatment for incarcerated women with substance abuse disorder and posttraumatic stress disorder: Findings from a pilot study. *Journal Sof Substance Abuse Treatment, 25*(2), 99-105.

doi:10.1300/J012v17n02_02

Research to Action:
Informing Policy Makers About the Needs
of Mothers and Children at Risk of Separation

Patricia E. Allard

SUMMARY. Over the past two decades, Congress has helped states develop demonstration projects enabling mothers at risk of incarceration for drug offenses to be diverted to community-based facilities to serve their sentence. Many of these projects allow mothers to live with their children while serving their sentence and completing a treatment program. While these demonstration projects are a step in the right direction, there are not enough of them to address the growing needs of mothers at risk of incarceration and children at risk of placement in foster care. With concentrated and thorough research assessing the effectiveness and possibilities for improvement of current demonstration projects, researchers can help demonstrate that it is sound for policy makers to move toward a nation-wide implementation of comprehensive

Patricia Allard is an Associate Counsel in the Criminal Justice Program at the Brennan Center for Justice at New York University Law School, 161 Avenue of the Americas, 12 FL, New York, NY 10013 (E-mail: Patricia.allard@nyu.edu). She is a graduate of Queen's University Law School (Canada) and received her MA in Criminology from the Center of Criminology at the University of Toronto. Patricia is a member of the American Society of Criminology.

Patricia owes a debt of gratitude to Andrea Ritchie for her incredibly thoughtful input in and editing of the article. Enormous thanks are given to Cecilia Lero for her support in the development, research and drafting of the article.

[Haworth co-indexing entry note]: "Research to Action: Informing Policy Makers About the Needs of Mothers and Children at Risk of Separation." Allard, Patricia E. Co-published simultaneously in *Women & Criminal Justice* (The Haworth Press, Inc.) Vol. 17, No. 2/3, 2006, pp. 27-42; and: *Drugs, Women, and Justice: Roles of the Criminal Justice System for Drug-Affected Women* (ed: James A. Swartz, Patricia O'Brien, and Arthur J. Lurigio) The Haworth Press, Inc., 2006, pp. 27-42. Single or multiple copies of this article are available for a fee from The Haworth Document Delivery Service [1-800-HAWORTH, 9:00 a.m. - 5:00 p.m. (EST). E-mail address: docdelivery@haworthpress.com].

community-based treatment programs for mothers and their children as an alternative to incarceration and foster care placement for families struggling with drug addiction. doi:10.1300/J012v17n02_03 *[Article copies available for a fee from The Haworth Document Delivery Service: 1-800-HAWORTH. E-mail address: <docdelivery@haworthpress.com> Website: <http://www.HaworthPress.com> © 2006 by The Haworth Press, Inc. All rights reserved.]*

KEYWORDS. Prison, treatment, women, mothers, children, sentencing, drugs, substance abuse, Adoption and Safe Families Act (ASFA), termination of parental rights, diversion, foster care, separation, non-violent offenses

INTRODUCTION

The number of women incarcerated in state and federal prisons has been climbing steadily since the 1980s. Existing research has shown that the criminalization of addiction and concomitant harsh sentencing schemes, central tactics in the "war on drugs," are the primary factors driving the rapid growth in the number of women, and particularly African-American and Latina women, in prisons (Frost, Greene & Pravis, 2006). As the number of women in prison increases, so do the number of children separated from their mothers due to incarceration (Mumola, 2000).

The passage of the Adoption and Safe Families Act of 1997 has increased the risk that many children and incarcerated mothers will be permanently separated as a result of the mother's imprisonment. Several studies have demonstrated the multiple negative impacts of separating parents and children, (Travis, Cincotta & Solomon, 2003) and suggest that maintenance of familial contact while women are incarcerated not only helps to prevent some of these impacts, but also aids formerly incarcerated women to reintegrate into their communities upon completion of their sentence (Acoca & Raeder, 2000; Kassebaum, 1999). Research has also shown that drug treatment programs can be effective alternatives to incarceration while, at the same time, permitting families to stay together (Hairston, Bates & Lawrence-Wills, 2003; Kassebaum, 1999).

Over the past two decades, Congress has provided funding to states to develop demonstration projects enabling mothers at risk of incarceration for non-violent drug offenses to be diverted to community-based facilities to serve their sentence. Many of these programs allow mothers to live either close to or with their children while serving their sentence and completing a drug treatment program. While these demonstration projects are a step in the right direction, they are currently insufficient in number and scope to address the growing needs of mothers at risk of incarceration and children at risk of placement in foster care and potentially permanent separation from their parents as a result of long sentences imposed for drug-related offenses. Two decades after their introduction, the continuing scarcity of available placements through such demonstration projects is no longer acceptable. Researchers have a responsibility to aid policy makers in moving beyond the status quo. With concentrated and thorough research assessing the effectiveness and possibilities for improvement of current initiatives, researchers can help advance a sound and comprehensive nationwide approach to the needs of mothers at risk of incarceration for non-violent drug offenses and their children.

The first section of this article lays out the criminal justice policies that have contributed to the growth in the number of mothers behind bars. Section two outlines how current child welfare policies further punish incarcerated mothers and their children and undermine the possibility of eventual family reunification, highlighting the urgency of developing alternative responses to substance abuse that will limit the separation of mothers and their children. The third section of the article documents policy makers' willingness, albeit limited, to divert mothers at risk of incarceration from prison to treatment programs, and advocates in favor of further steps in this direction. The article concludes that the development of a clearer understanding of which specific services and what implementation modalities make the most significant contribution to the treatment success of mothers with children is necessary to encourage policy makers to commit to the expansion of comprehensive family-based treatment programs.

IMPACTS OF CRIMINAL PUNISHMENT AND DRUG CONTROL POLICIES ON WOMEN WITH CHILDREN

The number of women in federal and state prisons has increased dramatically since the 1980s–there were 12,300 women behind bars in 1980, compared to over 105,000 in 2004 (Harrison & Beck, 2005). The "war on drugs" is the most significant contributing factor to the growth of the women's prison population, particularly for women of color.

Latinas and African-American women are most likely to be incarcerated for drug offenses. According to the most recent data available, 44% of Latinas and 39% of African-American women incarcerated in state prisons were convicted of a drug offense, whereas only 23% of white women, 24% of Black men, 26% of Latinos, and 11% of white men were incarcerated for drug offenses (Bureau of Justice Statistics, 2000).

The increasing number of women sentenced to prison for drug offenses has led to a dramatic growth in the number of children with an incarcerated mother. Between 1991 and 1999, the number of children with a mother in state or federal prison nearly doubled, increasing from 63,700 in 1991 to 126,100 in 1999 (Mumola, 2000).

The vast majority of offenses for which mothers are incarcerated are non-violent offenses. In 1997, three in four mothers were incarcerated for non-violent offenses–35% for drug offenses, 28% for property offenses (often drug-related), and 10% for public-order offenses (often also drug-related; Mumola, 2000). Existing research also indicates that most incarcerated mothers are more likely than fathers in prison to report past drug use, and in many cases, the offenses for which women are sentenced to correctional facilities are intricately related to their drug use. More than 86% of mothers in state prison had used drugs at some point in the past and 65% reported using drugs the month prior to their admission (Mumola, 2000). One third of mothers in state prison committed the crime for which they were incarcerated to get drugs or money for drugs, compared to a fifth of the fathers in prison (Mumola, 2000).

For many incarcerated women, drug use serves to numb the pain of years of physical, sexual or emotional abuse, as well as to help them to cope with the effects of racism, poverty and mental illness. (American Civil Liberties Union [ACLU], 2005; Richie, 1996). The lack of treatment programs that effectively address women's needs has been identified as an important contributor to women's continued drug use and, ultimately, contact with the criminal justice system. Indeed, the U.S. Substance Abuse and Mental Health Services Administration (SAMHSA) found that women accounted for only 33% of all substance abuse treatment admissions nation-wide in 2003 (Substance Abuse and Mental Health Services Administration [SAMHSA], 2003). Only 8% of available drug treatment programs provided childcare (SAMHSA, 2003).

Although it has been found to be more costly and less effective than comprehensive drug treatment, the punitive model continues to dominate states' interventions in substance-using women's lives. Over the past two decades strict sentencing guidelines, mandatory minimums, statutory enhancements for repeat offenders–such as "three strikes" and "truth in sentencing" laws[1] have been used as tools to implement a national mandate to stamp out drug use, significantly contributing to increased prison populations in both state and federal jurisdictions (Acoca & Raeder, 2000). Under these policies, the average maximum sentence length was 32 months for a drug offense and 28 months for a property offense for individuals incarcerated in 2002 (Bureau of Justice Statistics, 2005).

Under determinate sentencing schemes, little consideration is given to people's individual backgrounds and social responsibilities, or to the seriousness or extent of their involvement in illegal activity. As more and more women are incarcerated for drug offenses, a growing number of children and dependent adults[2] are left behind (ACLU, 2005). Current drug sentencing schemes translate to separation of more parents from their children for longer periods of time, resulting in serious emotional and psychological harm to both mothers and children. For instance, a 2003 study found that

> [t]he immediate effects [of parental separation due to imprisonment] can include feelings of shame, social stigma, loss of financial support, weakened ties to parents, changes in family composition, poor school performance, increased delinquency, and increased risk of abuse or neglect. Long-term effects can range from the questioning of parental authority, negative perceptions of police and the legal system, and increased dependency or maturational regression to impaired ability to cope with future stress or trauma, disruption of development, and intergenerational patterns of criminal behavior. (Travis, Cincotta & Solomon, 2003, p. 2)

While children feel these effects with either an incarcerated father or mother, children of incarcerated mothers are more likely to be uprooted from their homes because women are more often the primary caretakers of children prior to incarceration. In 1997, 44% of fathers in state prison and 55% in federal prison lived with their child or children at time of admission, compared to 64% of mothers in state prison and 84% of mothers in federal prison. Moreover, children are three times more likely to live with the other parent when fathers are incarcerated: of fathers behind bars, 90% in state prison and 92% in federal prison reported their children's current caregiver to be the mother. Only 28% of mothers in state prison and 31% in federal prison reported their children's current caregiver was the father. Children of incarcerated mothers are therefore three to five times more likely than children of incarcerated fathers to be placed in a foster home or agency (Mumola, 2000). As a result, when mothers are incarcerated, there is an increased risk that their families will become enmeshed in the child welfare system, placing them at greater risk of permanent separation. Given the non-violent and addiction-related nature of the offenses for which the vast majority of women are incarcerated, mothers are unnecessarily spending time in prison instead of receiving comprehensive support to address the socioeconomic and health issues that drive their addictions while continuing to care for their children, and the societal costs of current harsh drug sentencing policies are borne not only by parents, but also by their dependent children, and in some cases, by entire families.

In light of the wide-ranging adverse impacts of this approach, policy makers must reconsider the soundness of determinate sentencing as a means of addressing drug offenses. Rather than tying judges' hands at sentencing by imposing mandatory sentences for non-violent drug of-fenses, perhaps a more sound sentencing model would instead delineate the contours of judicial discretion, enabling judges to divert more peo-ple whose offenses do not warrant prison terms to community-based support programs such as drug treatment, thereby placing them in a better position to continue to attend to their social responsibilities in their communities while confronting substance abuse. While growth in the number of drug courts seeking to implement such an approach is perceived by many as a step in the right direction, the absence of drug treatment programs that meet the needs of women with children, and particularly of women who are survivors of sexual abuse and domestic violence, as well as the underlying punitive model of such courts, limits their effectiveness. Additionally, drug courts often do not offer support for family preservation and meeting parental obligations, reflecting a broader trend toward punishment of women with substance abuse is-sues as bad mothers rather than offering them support in the face of challenges that will enable them to better care for their children.

CHILD WELFARE POLICY AND INCARCERATED MOTHERS

The passage of the Adoption and Safe Families Act of 1997 (ASFA) increased the risk of permanent family dissolution for incarcerated mothers and their children. Through this Act, Congress sought to more quickly and safely move children from foster care to permanent or adoptive homes (Adoption and Safe Families Act [ASFA], 1997). To meet this new legislative mandate, policy makers directed states to make decisions concerning children in their care within shorter timelines. There are two timelines under ASFA that particularly affect incarcerated mothers and their children: (1) the Act requires states to hold a permanency hearing 12 months after the child enters foster care; and (2) ASFA mandates states to move for termination of parental rights (TPR) if a child has been in foster care for 15 of the most recent 22 months (Social Security Act, 2000).

During a permanency hearing the state determines whether and/or when the child will be returned to the parent, or if the child will be placed for adoption and parental rights will be terminated (Social Security Act, 2000). In order to avoid permanent separation from their children at this juncture, it is critical for mothers to maintain regular contact with their children and work with caseworkers to plan for the future and well-being of their children. In other words, notwithstanding incarceration, mothers must demonstrate their willingness and ability to be involved in their children's lives during the first 12 months of the child's placement in foster care to ensure the continuation of family reunification as a permanency plan.

Unfortunately, prison environments are not conducive to meeting the obligations the state imposes on mothers seeking to meet this requirement, and in many cases it is impossible for them to do so due to logistical barriers. For instance, many mothers are incarcerated far away from their children, limiting, and in some cases precluding, necessary visits with their children (Mumola, 2000). The costs of telephone communication may be so prohibitive that foster parents may be unable or unwilling to facilitate regular calls between mothers and their children (Stuart, 2005). Moreover, mothers in prison have limited phone privileges, thus limiting opportunities to communicate with their child's caseworker or others who may play a role in their child's life (Correctional Association of New York, 2006). Under such conditions of confinement, mothers are likely to face significant obstacles to demonstrating their bond with, and commitment to, the well-being of their children. Without adequate support and cooperation from state agencies, foster parents, relatives and friends, mothers are unlikely to be able to convince the state that there are "compelling reasons" not to terminate their parental rights, and that doing so would not be in the best interest of the child.

Although states are statutorily required to make "reasonable efforts" to reunify families, incarcerated mothers may not receive adequate reunification services. ASFA does not provide directives or guidelines as to the nature and scope of states' obligations to make reasonable efforts to provide family reunification services that meet the particular needs of incarcerated mothers and their children. Even in states such as California and New York, where mandated reunification services for incarcerated parents are outlined in state statutes, courts have been known to permanently sever parental rights even when child welfare agencies have not made reasonable efforts towards family reunification. As noted by the Correctional Association of New York (2006), "In practice…when the parent is incarcerated, child welfare agencies often fail to fulfill their responsibilities to make these mandated [reasonable efforts] and courts sometimes overlook serious breaches of permanency planning requirements in the interest of expediting adoptions" (p. 11). Incarcerated mothers are not only racing against time, they are also dealing with state agencies often ill-equipped to help them, and in some cases must struggle against strongly held beliefs concerning the fitness of women with substance abuse issues to be parents (Bean, 2005). Moreover, the financial incentives for states to make children available for adoption are great. Under ASFA, states receive financial bonuses between $4,000 and $6,000 per child for every child adopted beyond an established baseline (Social Security Act, 2000).

States may decline to file for termination of parental rights when a child is in the care of a relative (Social Security Act, 2000). However, it is important to note that such placements do not reset or halt the clock under ASFA; they only postpone the possibility of a TPR proceeding. As 80% of incarcerated mothers report their children are being cared for by grandparents or relatives, this TPR exception has been identified as increasing the possibility of post-release family reunification for incarcerated mothers and their children (Mumola, 2000). However, unfortunately, if for any reason, such as health or financial constraints, a child is moved from the care of a relative to that of a non-relative, the state can immediately move to terminate parental rights without being required to make reasonable efforts to reunify mother and child.

Pursuant to a Congressional directive, the Department of Health and Human Services (HHS) examined the impacts of ASFA on parents confronting substance abuse. HHS reported that "families involved in the child welfare and substance abuse treatment systems, and who are often involved with other service providers as well, face a variety of time constraints that may be at odds with one another" (U.S. Department of Health and Human Services, 1999, p. 72). Although HHS did not consider the particular circumstances of substance abusing parents incarcerated for drug or drug-related offenses in its study, it is clear that incarcerated mothers face additional time constraints. A recent study suggests that "ASFA has had an important effect" on incarcerated parents, based on "the significant overall increase" between 1997 and 2002 in the number of cases in which the parental rights have been terminated permanently (Lee, 2005). Since mothers sentenced by state or federal courts serve, on average, prison sentences longer than 15 months, meeting ASFA's timelines is likely to prove to be impossible based solely on their incarceration. As a result, a mandatory sentence of incarceration for a drug offense may automatically carry with it a life sentence of permanently losing one's child. When sentence length is combined with barriers to finding housing, a steady income, and combating addiction upon release from prison, the odds of avoiding termination of parental rights are even lower. Moreover, upon release, mothers with a drug conviction may face a number of post-conviction penalties, including, a lifetime ban on the receipt of welfare benefits in some states, inadmissibility to public housing, and exclusion from a variety of jobs and occupations requiring licenses (Allard, 2002).

OPPORTUNITIES TO DIVERT MOTHERS AT RISK OF INCARCERATION

Through their legislative directives in the last decade, many Congress members have acknowledged the necessity to address the needs of families struggling with substance abuse and child welfare, and in some cases, the needs of those enmeshed in the criminal justice system. Yet, during the deliberations preceding the passage of ASFA, Congress missed a timely opportunity for much needed reform. The SAFE Act, an early Senate version of ASFA, included very detailed and thoughtful provisions addressing the need for coordination of substance abuse treatment and child welfare systems, including appropriation recommendations for drug treatment programs (Safe Adoptions and Family Environments Act, 1997). For instance, one provision allowed for funds that would normally be allocated to foster care to be paid to residential drug treatment programs for children living with parents in treatment (Allen, M. L., 1997). In addition, Congress earmarked funds for 10 state demonstration projects, requiring states to give particular consideration to proposals from child welfare agencies that addressed substance use issues.

However, unfortunately, the SAFE Act did not address the needs of substance abusing mothers at risk of incarceration. In the end, ASFA provisions were limited to directing HHS to examine the needs of families struggling with substance abuse who come to the attention of child welfare agencies (U.S. Department of Health and Human Services, 1999).

Most recently, the USA PATRIOT Improvement and Reauthorization Act of 2005 authorized funds to develop demonstration projects addressing the unique needs of pregnant or parenting women potentially facing incarceration due to methamphetamine abuse (USA PATRIOT Improvement and Reauthorization Act of 2005). A state's application for funds under this provision must contain a description of family treatment programs to be administered if clinically appropriate, and if not appropriate, cross-agency family reunification services to be provided (USA PATRIOT Improvement and Reauthorization Act of 2005). This emphasis on promotion of "family permanence and self sufficiency," particularly in the substance abuse recovery process, is a very positive step. But much more can be done. Methamphetamine is but one drug among many substances leading to parental addiction and incarceration (Mumola, 2000). To have any hope of making a serious dent in the "war on drugs," Congress must make family-based treatment an alternative to incarceration available to parents dealing with *all forms of* substance abuse who are at risk of incarceration for non-violent offenses.

In 1994, a similar but more comprehensive law, the Family Unity Demonstration Project Act, was introduced as part of the Violent Crime Control and Law Enforcement Act of 1994 (Raeder, 2000). Unlike the demonstration project initiative under the PATRIOT ACT, this statute would have allowed parents convicted of any non-violent offense to live with children in residential facilities instead of prison or jail (Family Unity Demonstration Project Act, 1994). Although Congress passed the Family Unity Demonstration Project Act in 1994 and authorized between $3.6 and $5.4 million annually from fiscal year 1996 through fiscal year 2000 for its implementation, no funds were actually appropriated for such programs (Raeder, 2000). In 2000, the American Bar Association recommended reauthorization and full funding of the Act, stating "The creation of additional community correctional facilities for nonviolent mothers would ensure the maintenance of strong family ties and keep children from being placed outside their home...[the projects] would have constituted a positive step towards bettering the lives of parents whose crimes did not warrant imprisonment that separates them from their children" (Raeder, 2000).

These legislative efforts demonstrate that Congressional members responsible for child welfare matters recognize the interconnectedness of substance use and child neglect or abuse. Unfortunately, these legislative efforts have continually fallen short of confronting and addressing the needs of incarcerated mothers convicted of non-violent drug offenses and their children.[3] Although demonstration projects dealing with substance abuse, criminal punishment and child welfare matters represent a step in the right direction, it is time for Congress and state legislatures to collaborate to address systematically the needs of mothers at risk of incarceration for nonviolent offenses through measures including comprehensive family-based treatment.

THE NEED FOR TREATMENT EXPANSION

Researchers and advocates have increasingly identified treatment as a superior alternative to incarceration for individuals struggling with substance abuse (Acoca & Raeder, 2001; Daley, Argeriou, McCarty, Callahan, Shephard & Williams, 2000; Mitchell, 1993). However, a more complete understanding of the treatment services and modalities that are effective for mothers and their children is needed. The Center for Substance Abuse Treatment (CSAT), a division of HHS, asserts that addicted women "can be helped through comprehensive programs designed specifically for women, treating the factors associated with substance abuse" (Kassebaum, 1999, p. 3). Comprehensive substance abuse treatment requires a "continuum of services that promotes recovery and enables the substance abuse client to fully integrate into society as a healthy, substance-free individual. The continuum must be designed to provide engagement and motivation, primary treatment services at the appropriate intensity and level, and support services that will enable the individual to maintain long-term sobriety while managing life in the community" (Siegal, 1998).

Cultural sensitivity is another key element of comprehensive treatment programs. It is important to building the trust and community-like atmosphere necessary for comprehensive treatment, ensuring participants' full attention and commitment to recovery. Mothers with substance abuse problems are often viewed as villains, and cultural disparities and racial stereotypes may exacerbate this perception. Moreover, service providers and clients may disagree about effective programming events and parenting goals (Baker & Carson, 1999). Further development and comparative evaluations of culturally appropriate programming (Bass, 1997) are necessary to better assess their importance in a nationwide framework for comprehensive drug treatment and to develop effective programming for diverse women.

Available evidence confirms that effective treatment programs empower women to stop the cycle of substance abuse and crime, and become more productive members of their communities. Not only are women and their children greatly benefited, but further investment in treatment programs would result in "enormous savings for U.S. society...It costs considerably less to treat a woman than to build a jail cell to incarcerate her or to pay for foster care placement for her child (Kassebaum, p. 3; see also Daley et. al., 2000, p. 445).

In 1993, CSAT convened a Consensus Panel of medical and substance treatment experts, social service providers and representatives of national organizations to publish a Treatment Improvement Protocol (TIP) providing directives on how to best support pregnant substance-using women and their families. Key guidelines emerging from the Panel's consultative process focused on meeting individual needs, and were placed in a strong, overarching framework based on the understanding that use of alcohol and drugs is "a public health issue, not a legal problem." The Panel concluded that it "does not support the criminal prosecution of pregnant, substance-using women. Furthermore, there is no evidence that punitive approaches work" (Mitchell, 1993). Instead, the Panel recommended comprehensive medical care and treatment for addiction, including the long-term provision of services, viewing these as essential to start substance-abusing women on the road to recovery. The Panel concluded that "[t]his approach, it is hoped, will result in more productive adults, stronger families, and healthier children" (Mitchell, 1993).

However, despite these government-sanctioned recommendations, comprehensive treatment options are still the exception rather than the rule. There remains a conspicuous lack of treatment centers that admit pregnant women and/or women with children, and treat them in a gender-sensitive framework. As of January 3, 2005, "CSAT funded approximately 514 active grantees providing direct services. Of these, 105 (20 percent) serve only women or include women as a primary target population." Of these 105 programs, 20 (19%) serve pregnant and postpartum women, or offer residential treatment for women and their children (Treatment Improvement Exchange, 2005; see Center for Substance Abuse Treatment, 2006; Kumpfer, 1991; Stahler, G. J., Shipley, Jr., T. E., Kirby, K. C., Godboldte, C., Kerwin, M. E., Shandler et al., 2005). Moreover, women are often reluctant to enter the few programs that do exist for fear of being prosecuted for drug use and/or losing custody of their children (Baker, 2000).

Studies to date have shown that the encouragement and preservation of family ties are important to rehabilitation during both imprisonment and drug treatment (Hairston, 1988; Gregoire & Schultz, 2001). The ability of a child to reside with his or her mother during treatment is particularly critical. Separation from a parent, no matter the cause, can result in a serious sense of loss for the child, who may exhibit symptoms of Post-Traumatic Stress Disorder, including depression, feelings of anger, and guilt (Hagan & Dinovitzer, 1999). Allowing children to reside with their mothers during treatment addresses the obstacle, faced by many mothers struggling with substance abuse, of finding adequate childcare or an alternate caregiver, while also allowing the child to receive support in connection with stresses arising from his or her mother's substance abuse while the mother is simultaneously receiving treatment. CSAT recognizes that there is not only a shortage, but also inadequate delivery of services within comprehensive residential treatment programs for women and their children, (CSAT, 2006; Kumpfer, 1991; Stahler, et. al., 2005) and recommends a more systematic approach to service delivery in order to address the problems created by the current fragmented approach. A systematic approach would help enable policymakers to close gaps in the service delivery system and facilitate the improvement of existing programs and the creation of new programs.

However, according to the Institute of Medicine, empirical research confirms a gap between research and treatment practice (Heinrich & Fournier, 2005). An effective systematic approach is unfeasible if assessments of existing programs are lacking or are not readily available to inform the development of future programs. While it may be difficult to quantitatively assess the impacts of particular program elements within a universal treatment program, qualitative studies of the perceived effectiveness or utility of particular modalities or frameworks would prove useful to that end. Development of a clearer understanding of which specific services and what implementation modalities make the most significant contribution to treatment success is necessary if we are to have a clear understanding of what truly constitutes "comprehensive" treatment, and which effective programming areas should be improved and expanded. To be sure, there have been a number of national studies assessing the effectiveness of residential drug treatment, however, in order to move Congress towards implementing a national comprehensive treatment initiative that meets the needs of women, and particularly of mothers, struggling with substance abuse, more targeted program assessment research is needed to evaluate particular program elements aimed at addressing these needs.

CONCLUSION

In many fields and contexts, social science research has proven helpful to assisting policy makers in identifying, understanding, and rectifying social problems. At the current juncture, as a growing number of women are incarcerated for non-violent drug or drug-related offenses, the majority of whom are mothers who, under the Adoption and Safe Families Act, are at risk of being permanently separated from their children, research is once again urgently needed to assist policy makers in identifying the elements of a nationwide strategy to address the needs of individuals struggling with substance abuse. Unfortunately, insufficient research has been done to date to guide Congress members and state legislators towards effective solutions addressing the needs of mothers dealing with substance abuse and who are enmeshed in both the criminal justice and child welfare systems. Under these circumstances, researchers have a responsibility to conduct directed research that will inform policy makers how to best reform the current criminal and child welfare law laws that place families at risk of permanent separation, at significant cost to individuals, families, and society. And broad-based, holistic, and wide-ranging reform is clearly needed to give families struggling with substance abuse a fighting chance to heal.

NOTES

1. Truth in Sentencing laws are those that are designed to limit early parole by mandating that incarcerated people serve a certain percentage (such as 85%) of their sentence before they are released on parole.

2. An estimated 24,000 women nation-wide provided to dependent adults prior to incarceration.

3. One exception is found in "Promoting Safe and Stable Families Amendments," Pub. L 107-133 on January 17, 2002. However, the provisions amending ASFA are limited to mentoring programs for children of incarcerated parents.

REFERENCES

Acoca, L., & Raeder, M. S. (2000). Severing family ties: The plight of nonviolent female offenders and their children. *Stanford Law & Policy Review, 11*, 133-151.

Allard, P. (2002). *Life sentences: Denying welfare benefits to women convicted of drug offenses*. Washington, DC: The Sentencing Project.

Allen, M. L. (Speaker). (1997). *Adoption Promotion Act of 1997: Hearing on H.R. 867 before the Senate Subcomm. On Human Resources,* 105th Cong. 105-10.

American Civil Liberties Union, Break the Chains: Communities of Color and the War on Drugs & the Brennan Center for Justice at NYU School of Law. (2005). *Caught in the Net: The Impact of Drug Policies on Women and Families.* New York: Authors.

Baker, P. L., & Carson, A. (1999). I take care of my kids: Mothering practices of substance-abusing women. *Gender & Society, 13,* 347-363.

Baker, P. L. (2000). I didn't know: Discoveries and identity transformation of women addicts in treatment. *Journal of Drug Issues, 30,* 863-881.

Bass, L. (1997). A study of drug abusing African-American pregnant women. *Journal of Drug Issues, 27,* 659-671.

Bean, K. S. (2005). Reasonable efforts: What state courts think. *Toledo Law Review, 36,* 321-366.

Bureau of Justice Statistics (2005). *Criminal Sentencing Statistics.* Retrieved April 5, 2006, from http://www.ojp.usdoj.gov/bjs/sent.htm#findings.

Bureau of Justice Statistics (2000). Survey of inmates in state and federal correctional facilities. In *Correctional Populations in the United States, 1997* (NCJ 177613). Washington, DC: Author.

Cal. Penal Code § 1174.4.

Cal. Penal Code § 1174.9.

Center for Substance Abuse Treatment (n.d.). *Program overview: Welcome to the PIC website home page.* Retrieved April 5, 2006, from http://csat.samhsa.gov/pic/index.html.

Correctional Association of New York, Women in Prison Project. (2006). *When "free' means losing your mother: the collision of child welfare and the incarceration of women in New York State.* New York, NY: Author.

Daley, M., Argeriou, M., McCarty, D., Callahan, Jr., J. J., Shepard, D. S., & Williams, C. N. (2000). The costs of crime and the benefits of substance abuse treatment for pregnant women. *Journal of Substance Abuse Treatment, 19,* 445-458.

Family Unity Demonstration Project Act, 42 U.S.C. §§ 13881-13882.

Frost, N. A., Greene, J., & Pranis, K. (2006). *Hard hit: The Growth in the imprisonment of women, 1977-2004.* New York, NY: Women's Prison Association.

Gregoire, K. A. & Schultz, D. (2001). Substance-abusing child welfare parents: Treatment and child placement outcomes. *Child Welfare, 80,* 433-453.

Hagan, J., & Dinovitzer, R. (1999). Collateral consequences of imprisonment for children, communities and prisoners. *Crime and Justice, 26,* 121-162.

Hairston, C. F. (1988). Family ties during imprisonment: Do they influence future criminal activity? *Federal Probation, 52,* 48-52.

Hairston, C. F., Bates, R. E., & Lawrence-Wills, S. (2003). Serving incarcerated mothers and their babies in community-based residences. *Research Brief: Children, Families, and the Criminal Justice System.* Chicago, Illinois: University of Illinois at Chicago, Jane Addams Center for Social Policy and Research.

Harrison, P. M., & Beck, A. J. (2005). *Prisoners in 2004.* Bureau of Justice Statistics: Bulletin. U.S. Department of Justice. October.

Kassebaum, P. A. (1999). *Substance abuse treatment for women offenders. Guide to promising practices: TIP 23* [Electronic version]. (DHHS Publication No. 99-3303).

Rockville, MD: U.S. Department of Health and Human Services, Center for Substance Abuse Treatment.

Kumpfer, K. L. (1991). Treatment programs for drug-abusing women. *The Future of Children, 1*, 50-60.

Lee, A. F., Genty, P. M., & Laver M. (2005). The Impact of the Adoption and Safe Families Act on children of incarcerated parents. Washington, D.C.: Child Welfare League of America.

Mitchell, J. L. (1993) *Pregnant substance-using women: Treatment Improvement Protocol (TIP) Series 2* [Electronic version]. (DHHS Publication No. SMA 95-3056). Rockville, MD: U.S. Department of Health and Human Services, Center for Substance Abuse Treatment.

Mumola, C. J. (2000). *Incarcerated parents and their children.* Bureau of Justice Statistics: Special Report. Washington, DC: U.S. Department of Justice.

N.D. Cent. Code § 19-03.1 (2005).

Raeder, M. S. (2000). Sentencing symposium: Creating correctional alternatives for nonviolent women offenders and their children. *St. Louis Law Journal, 44*, 377.

Richie, B. (1996). Compelled to crime: the gender entrapment of battered black women. London: Routledge.

Safe Adoptions and Family Environments Act (SAFE Act), S. 511, 105th Cong. (1997).

Siegal, Harvey A. (1998). *Comprehensive case management for substance abuse treatment: TIP 27* [Electronic version]. (DHHS Publication No. SMA 98-3222) Rockville, MD: U.S. Department of Health and Human Services, Center for Substance Abuse Treatment.

Social Security Act, 42 U.S.C. § 675 (5)(C)-(E) (2000).

Stahler, G. J., Shipley, Jr., T. E., Kirby, K. C., Godboldte, C., Kerwin, M. E., Shandler, I. et al. (2005). Development and initial demonstration of a community-based intervention for homeless, cocaine-using African-American women. *Journal of Substance Abuse Treatment, 28*, 171-179.

Stuart, C. (2005, January 7). Groups Fight N.Y. State Prison Collect Call 'Kickbacks' [Electronic version]. *The New Standard.*

Substance Abuse and Mental Health Services Administration (SAMHSA) (2003). *National Survey of Substance Abuse Treatment Services.* Retrieved April 10, 2006, from http://wwwdasis.samhsa.gov/webt/state_data/US03.pdf.

Travis, J., Cincotta, E. M., & Solomon, A. L. (October 2003). *Families left behind: The hidden costs of incarceration and reentry* [Electronic version]. Washington, DC: Urban Institute Justice Policy Center.

Treatment Improvement Exchange. (2005, January 5). Overview of CSAT grantees providing treatment services to women. Retrieved April 5, 2006 from http://womenandchildren.treatment.org/media/misc/WomensDiscretionaryReport.doc.

U.S. Department of Health and Human Services. (1999). *Blending perspectives and building common ground.* Washington, DC: U.S. Government Printing Office.

USA PATRIOT Improvement and Reauthorization Act of 2005, Pub. L. No. 109-177 § 756 (2006).

doi:10.1300/J012v17n02_03

Differences Among Children Whose Mothers Have Been in Contact with the Criminal Justice System

Susan D. Phillips

Alaattin Erkanli

E. Jane Costello

Adrian Angold

SUMMARY. In order to effectively help children whose mothers become involved with the criminal justice system, it is important to understand their differing needs. To that end, the analyses described in this article explore the heterogeneity in parent and family risks among a group of children whose mothers had contact with the criminal justice system. Using data from an epidemiologic study of youth, results showed that the two most prevalent problems in the backgrounds of this group of youth were poverty (61.5%) and maternal mental health problems (54.9%). But, results of cluster analyses suggest this group is actually made up of

Dr. Susan D. Phillips, PhD, is Assistant Professor at Jane Addams College of Social Work, University of Illinois at Chicago. Dr. Alaattin Erkanli, PhD, is Assistant Research Professor of Biometry, Dr. E. Jane Costello, PhD, is Professor of Medical Psychology, and Dr. Adrian Angold, MRCPsych, is Associate Professor of Psychiatry and Behavioral Sciences, Developmental Epidemiology Program, Department of Psychiatry and Behavioral Science, Duke University Medical Center.

Address correspondence to: Dr. Susan Phillips, PhD, Jane Addams College of Social Work M/C 309, 1040 W. Harrison St., Chicago, IL 60607 (E-mail: suephi@uic.edu).

[Haworth co-indexing entry note]: "Differences Among Children Whose Mothers Have Been in Contact with the Criminal Justice System." Phillips, Susan D. et al. Co-published simultaneously in *Women & Criminal Justice* (The Haworth Press, Inc.) Vol. 17, No. 2/3, 2006, pp. 43-61; and: *Drugs, Women, and Justice: Roles of the Criminal Justice System for Drug-Affected Women* (ed: James A. Swartz, Patricia O'Brien, and Arthur J. Lurigio) The Haworth Press, Inc., 2006, pp. 43-61. Single or multiple copies of this article are available for a fee from The Haworth Document Delivery Service [1-800-HAWORTH, 9:00 a.m. - 5:00 p.m. (EST). E-mail address: docdelivery@haworthpress.com].

Available online at http://wcj.haworthpress.com
© 2006 by The Haworth Press, Inc. All rights reserved.
doi:10.1300/J012v17n02_04

four meaningfully different subgroups: (1) children with only isolated risks, (2) children with histories of abuse, (3) children who have multiple parents/caregivers with histories of drug abuse and/or mental health problems, and (4) children whose parents have few problems, but who are living in economically deprived, single-parent households. doi:10.1300/ J012v17n02_04 *[Article copies available for a fee from The Haworth Document Delivery Service: 1-800-HAWORTH. E-mail address: <docdelivery@ haworthpress.com> Website: <http://www.HaworthPress.com> © 2006 by The Haworth Press, Inc. All rights reserved.]*

KEYWORDS. Arrest, incarceration, unintended consequences, delinquency, prevention

INTRODUCTION

The expansion of the criminal justice system over the past two decades raised concerns about the possible adverse consequences for children stemming from the greater involvement of criminal justice authorities in the lives of parents–particularly mothers (e.g.,, Johnston & Carlin, 1996). Mothers account for only a relatively small proportion of individuals involved in the criminal justice system, but the arrest of mothers, particularly when it results in incarceration, is believed to be more disruptive to children than the arrest or incarceration of fathers (Koban, 1983). This is because mothers who are taken into custody are more likely than fathers to be their children's sole primary caregiver (Smith & Elstein, 1994) and their children are more likely to live with grandparents (Mullen, 1995). This is a cause for concern because the grandparents caring for these children may have limited financial means (Bloom & Steinhart, 1993) and, at the same time, public assistance programs that are available to parents are not always accessible to grandparents (Phillips & Bloom, 1998). A further concern is that the arrest of mothers sometimes results in children being taken into custody by child welfare authorities, placed in foster homes, and, in the end, may result in the termination of mothers' parental rights (Beckerman, 1998; Ross, Khashu & Wamsley, 2004; Smith & Elstein, 1994; see also Allard, this volume).

In the wake of record growth in the number of mothers under criminal justice supervision, advocates, journalists, and researchers have been attempting to document what happens to the children whose mothers become involved in the criminal justice system. These efforts include describing children's experiences at various junctures as mothers progress through the criminal justice system (e.g., Bernstein, 2005); learning about how mother-child relationships are affected by incarceration (e.g., Poehlmann, 2005); assessing the service needs of mothers, their children, and relative caregivers (e.g., Smith, Krisman, Strozler & Marley, 2004); and examining the overlap between children whose parents are involved in the criminal justice system and child service populations (e.g., Phillips, Burns, Wagner, Kramer & Robbins, 2002; Phillips, Burns, Wagner & Barth, 2004).

Be it their father or mother, there is potential for children to be adversely affected by problems parents have that may have contributed to their parent's arrest. For example, women in the criminal justice system have higher rates of addictions and mental health problems than are normally found among women in the general population (e.g., Abram, Teplin & McClelland, 2003). In turn, there is considerable evidence linking these maternal problems with an elevated risk of youth developing serious emotional and behavioral problems such as delinquency, substance abuse, and psychopathology (Costello, Farmer, Angold, Burns & Erkanli,1997; Giancola, 2000; Loukas, Fitzgerald, Zucker & Eye, 2001).

One of the ways in which maternal substance abuse and mental illness can influence the development of serious youth problems is through their impact on children's family circumstances. Adverse family circumstance, or family risks, associated with the development of serious problems include single-parent households, poverty, inadequate parenting (e.g., lack of supervision, overly harsh or punitive discipline), family instability, and physical and sexual abuse. There is a greater probability of finding these circumstances in homes where there is maternal substance abuse or mental illness than in homes where mothers do not have these problems (e.g., Ammerman, Kolko, Kirisci, Blackson & Dawes, 1999; Keller, Catalono, Haggerty & Fleming, 2002; Kupersmidt, Griesler, DeRosier, Patterson & Davis, 1995).

At the same time, accounts of the experiences of children following maternal arrest or during periods of maternal incarceration suggest that the arrest and incarceration of mothers also affects children's family lives. For instance, the arrest of a mother can result in children being separated from their sole primary caregiver (Sharp, 2004), contribute to short- and long-term economic hardship (Allard, 2002), and lead to residential and caregiver instability (Stanton, 1980). There has also been theorizing about how these conditions combine to affect the ability of caregivers to adequately meet children's emotional and material needs (Johnston & Carlin, 1996).

There are many notable limitations to this body of literature (i.e., reliance on convenience samples, use of non-standardized measures, second-hand accounts of children's status) (Johnston, 1995; Murray & Farrington, 2005; Phillips et al., 2002). Be that as it may, this research has played an important role in raising concerns about the adversities that some young people may endure when their mothers come under the supervision of criminal justice authorities. Moreover, it has given impetus to new correctional and community programs. In correctional settings, programs are being implemented to help parents sustain their relationships with their children, improve their parenting abilities, and make parent-child visitation a more constructive time (Carlson, 2001; Dickon, 2005; Kazura & Toth, 2004; National Institute of Corrections [NIC], 2002; Snyder, Carol & Coats Mullins, 2001). On "the outside," there are a growing number of support and service programs for children whose parents are involved with criminal authorities and the people caring for them, including a current federally supported effort to supply children of incarcerated parents with mentors (Mustin, D'Arville & Scmaltz-Reidt, 2005; Bush-Baskette & Patino, 2004; Slavin, 2004).

Service planning and development efforts, however, might benefit from exploring differences that may exist among children whose parents violate the law. A decade ago, Johnston (1995) pointed out that "even among groups of prisoners' children selected for study because of their emotional, behavioral, or disciplinary problems, few of the children had problems in every area and all of the children were performing adequately in one or more areas" (p. 63) Yet, as suggested by the terms "children of incarcerated parents" or "children of female offenders," the emphasis of research and advocacy has been on *between*-group differences; e.g., differences between children whose parents have and have not been arrested, or differences between children of men and women who are under the supervision of the criminal justice system.

Although the heterogeneity among children of offenders has not received much attention beyond describing differences between children of female and male offenders, or needs and concerns particular to children living with relatives or involved with child welfare authorities, there is reason to believe that there could be meaningful differences in prevention and intervention needs among children of offenders. For instance, the final report on federal demonstration projects for children of incarcerated parents noted that different types of supportive services may be indicated for children with parents serving life sentences versus those serving relatively short sentences (Bush-Baskette & Patino, 2004). Also, findings from the National Survey of Child and Adolescent Well-Being pointed out differences among children with arrested mothers in the child welfare system in the types of maltreatment they had experienced and the nature of their mother's problems (Phillips et al., 2004). Thus, although it has not been a focus of attention, there is evidence that children whose mothers become involved in the criminal justice system are not a homogenous group. Enumerating the differences that exist among these youth could lead to better preparation of program volunteers and staff and to programs that more accurately target the needs of this population.

METHODS

Sample Selection

The findings presented in this article are based on analyses of data from The Great Smoky Mountains Study (GSMS), a longitudinal epidemiologic study of youth from 11 rural counties in western North Carolina (Costello et al., 1996). The oldest GSMS participants were born in 1979 and 1980 and therefore grew up during a period in which the criminal justice system in North Carolina, like other states, underwent dramatic growth.

GSMS is based on an accelerated cohort design (Kleinbaum, Kupper & Morgenstern, 1982) in which youth ages 9, 11, and 13 were recruited into the study and then followed prospectively. The sampling frames were the information management systems of public school districts in the 11 participating counties and schools on the The Qualla Boundary, the home of the Eastern Band of the Cherokee Nation, which is also located in the target geographic area.

Youth from public school districts were selected using a two-stage sampling approach. In the first stage, a sample of 4,500 children was randomly selected using data from school districts' information management systems. A screening questionnaire based on the Child Behavior Checklist (CBCL; Achenbach & Edelbrock, 1981) was administered and, in the second stage, all children who scored above the 75th percentile on the CBCL plus a 10 percent sample of children with lower scores were recruited into the study ($n = 1073$).

To assure adequate representation of American Indian children, all eligible children from Qualla Boundary schools ($n = 431$) were invited to participate. A total of 347 (80 percent) took part in the study.

Combining the two samples results in 1,420 children who entered the study when they were ages 9, 11, or 13. Using the combined data, population estimates can be derived by applying sampling weights that adjust for the two-stage sample design (over-sampling youth with high screen scores) and the different selection criteria of the two samples (American Indian and other children). These weights are inversely proportional to the sampling probability for young people selected via the two-stage sampling and reflect the known population proportion of American Indians in the 11-county region.

The current analyses are based on a subset of 306 children (14.5%) of the GSMS population whose mothers had contact with criminal justice authorities. In terms of absolute numbers, 306 GSMS participants fell in this category.

Constructs and Measures

Parallel versions of the Child and Adolescent Psychiatric Assessment (CAPA) (Angold et al., 1995) were administered separately to children and an adult respondent. Data used in the present analyses are based on information from the family environment and life events sections of the CAPA (Costello, Angold, March & Fairbank, 1998).

Contact with the criminal justice system. Mothers' contact with the criminal justice system was established from responses to items inquiring about whether children's biological parents or other significant parent figures (e.g., adoptive parents, step-parents) had ever been arrested as an adult. Information was solicited about both parents/parent figures residing in and out of the home. If an arrest was reported, respondents were then asked if the parent/parent figure had been charged and, if so, the worst result of the charge. The possible choices of worst charge included: (1) arrested, but not charged, (2) arrested, but found not guilty, (3) fined, (4) community punishment (e.g., probation, community service, treatment order), and (5) detention (i.e., incarceration/house arrest). Incarceration and house arrest are a combined response category in the CAPA interview and consequently cannot be disentangled. However, we are mindful that these two types of sanctions may have very different consequences for youth.

Parent risks. The parent risk factors examined were parental substance abuse and parental mental health problems. Indicators of substance abuse and mental health problems were any report of parents/parent figures ever seeking or receiving treatment for these problems and, in the case of mental health, taking medications. The occurrence of parental substance abuse and mental health problems were measured across each child's lifespan (birth to age 16).

Family risks. Most measures of children's exposure to family risks pertained to the 3-month intervals preceding the baseline and subsequent annual interviews. Therefore, they pertain to the period between ages 9, 11, or 13 (baseline) up through 16. For purposes of presentation, family risk factors are grouped into five categories: (1) family composition, (2) household economic strains, (3) quality of care, (4) victimization of children, and (5) instability. The specific indicators associated with each of these categories are listed in Table 1.

TABLE 1. Family Risks and Associated Indicators

Family Composition	Economic Strains	Quality of Care	Victimization of Child	Instability
Single-caregiver household Foster placement* Size (4 or more children in home)	Household income below the federal poverty limit One or more unemployed caregivers in the home Reduced standard of living (e.g., family experienced an event which triggered the inability to pay utility bills or other financial obligations) Unable to meet children's basic needs for food, housing, clothing, and medical attention	Harsh or punitive parenting Lack of age appropriate child supervision Child treated as a scapegoat Over protective or intrusive parenting	Physically abused by a parent or parent figure* Sexually abused*	Residential instability (5 or more moves in a 5 year period) Parent-child separation (a parent or significant parent figure moved out of the home) New parent figure in household (e.g., parent remarried, a new partner moved into the home)

* The reference period for these risk Indicators is birth through age 16. For all other indicators, the reference period is age 9, 11, or 13 through age 16.

Analyses

Weighted population estimates from preliminary analyses showed that through age 16, approximately 14.5 percent of all children represented by GSMS data had a biological mother who had been arrested at least once. In terms of absolute numbers, this amounts to 306 children with mothers who had contact with the criminal justice system. Because of the relatively small absolute size of this group and because past analyses of GSMS data have shown that the 3-month population prevalence rates for some of the risk exposures of interest are relatively low (Costello et al., 1997), data were collapsed across observation periods to maximize the number of cases available for analyses. Analyses are therefore based on lifetime (or baseline through age 16) risk exposure rather than time-varying measures.

Furthermore, bivariate data were converted into counts of the number of risk factors reported in each of the five areas of family risks shown in Table 1. For parent problems (not shown), the range of possible scores was 0 to 6. This is a result of counting substance abuse and mental illness separately and counting reports for mothers, fathers, and other caregivers individually (2 problems x 3 categories of parent figure = 6).

Analytic approach. The heterogeneity of this subset of the GSMS sample was explored using cluster analyses, a class of methods for grouping individuals into unknown groups. To increase confidence in the reliability of the derived clusters, we used multiple hierarchical and disjoint clustering techniques, comparing the results for consensus. Analyses were executed using SAS Proc CLUSTER and SAS Proc FASTCLUS, respectively.

First, hierarchical clustering was carried out using three alternate methods for grouping cases: (1) average linkage, (2) Ward's method, and (3) centroids. The number of clusters suggested by these grouping methods was determined by examining where marked changes occurred in incremental differences in the cubic clustering criterion (CCC) (Sarle, 1983), the pseudo F statistic, and a distance ratio calculated by dividing the distance to the to the nearest cluster (root mean square [RMS] standard deviation) by the average within cluster distance. These different grouping methods suggested a three- or four-cluster solution.

Next, disjoint clustering was carried out using FASTCLUS, a SAS procedure using Euclidean distances that bases cluster centers on least-squares estimation (i.e., a k-means model). Given the results of the hierarchical clustering, both three and four clusters were alternately specified. Finally, discriminant function analysis was conducted to examine how well cluster membership differentiated among youth based on parent and family risks. The four-cluster solution was selected on the basis of its comparatively lower overall misclassification rate in the discriminant analyses (4 percent versus 13 percent for the 3-cluster solution).

RESULTS

Race/Ethnicity

African American youth were over-represented among children with arrested mothers. As Table 2 shows, African American youth made up less than 4 percent of the population represented by GSMS, but accounted for approximately 11 percent of youth whose mothers had a history of arrest during adulthood. American Indian youth were also over-represented, but to a lesser extent.

Parent/Parent Figure Contact with Criminal Authorities

Of the 14.5 percent of the population of youth represented by GSMS data whose mothers were arrested as adults, only 1 in 4 had only a mother with an arrest history (24.4%of children with arrested mothers). Approximately 2 out of 3 (68.0%) also had a father who had been arrested and about 1 in 5 had a parent figure other than a mother or father who was arrested (20.9%). Moreover, about 1 in 7 of these children (13.3%) had a mother, father, and other parent figure who had been arrested.

Worst Result of Contact with Criminal Authorities

Of the mothers who had contact with criminal authorities, approximately two-thirds were either never charged following their arrest, were

TABLE 2. Race/Ethnicity

Race/Ethnicity	Mother Had Contact with Criminal Justice System (%)	GSMS Population (%)
White	81.4	89.4
African American	11.1	3.7
American Indian	7.5	6.9

ultimately found not guilty, or received only a fine. Only 16.7 percent of these mothers had been incarcerated. In contrast, 41.0 percent of children whose mothers had contact with the criminal justice system had fathers who had been incarcerated (Table 3).

Prevalence of Parent and Family Risks

The five most common parent and family risk factors observed among all children in the GSMS population whose mothers had contact with the criminal justice system were residential instability (42.7 percent), caregiver unemployment (48.1 percent), single-caregiver homes (52.0 percent), maternal mental health problems (54.9 percent), and–the most pervasive risk–poverty (61.5 percent). There were other risk factors that were not as prevalent, but that were reported at much higher rates than one would expect in the general population. Among these were physical and sexual abuse and placement in foster care (Table 4).

Parent and Family Risk Subgroups

Results of cluster analyses suggested that children whose mothers had contact with criminal authorities can be classified into four groups based on parent and family risks. Cluster means based on the number of reported risks in each of the six categories of interest are shown in Table 5. Table 6 lists individual risks reported by 50 percent or more of youth in each cluster. Considering Table 5 and 6 together, the identified groups were characterized by: (1) isolated risks (52.8 percent), (2) history of abuse (14.7 percent), (3) pervasive parent problems (18.9 percent), and (4) economic deprivation and single-parent households (13.7 percent).

TABLE 3. Worst Result of Arrest (Percent of Children Whose Mothers Had Contact with the Criminal Justice System)

Worst Result	Mother %	Father %	Other Parent Figure %
Detention	16.7	41.0	9.2
Community Sanction	17.8	7.8	0.5
Fine	42.8	16.3	7.0
Not guilty	9.1	1.0	2.4
Not charged	14.0	2.0	1.8

TABLE 4. Prevalence and Mean Number of Parent and Family Risks

Risk Factor	Mother Had Contact with Criminal Justice System %	Other Children %
Parent Problems		
Parental Substance Abuse[a]		
Mother	16.0***	3.0
Father	20.3***	11.4
Other Parent Figure	10.4***	4.9
Mental Illness*		
Mother	54.9***	37.9
Father	31.0***	20.0
Other Parent Figure	19.2***	8.7
Mean # (std) of above (0-6)	1.5 (0.9)***	0.9 (1.1)
Family Risks		
Family Composition		
Single-caregiver	52.0***	32.3
Foster care[a]	13.6***	7.1
Large size (4 or more sibling in household)	15.2***	3.1
Mean # (std) of above (0-3)	0.8(0.7)***	0.4(0.6)
Economic Strains		
Income below poverty level	61.5***	29.4
Unemployed caregiver	48.1***	26.3
Reduced standard of care	23.5***	11.9
Unable to meet children's basic needs	36.5***	13.4
Mean # (std) of above (0-4)	1.7 (0.9)8***	0.8(1.0)
Quality of Care		
Harsh or punitive parenting	3.5	2.6
Lack of supervision	36.0***	22.2
Child treated as a scapegoat	3.8	3.6
Over protective or intrusive parenting	5.4**	1.9
Mean # (std) of above (0-4)	0.5(0.5)***	0.3(0.6)
Victimization of Child		
Physically abused by parent[a]	12.8***	5.6
Sexual abuse[a]	18.0***	9.8
Mean # (std) of above (0-2)	0.3(0.4)***	0.2(0.4)
Instability		
Residential instability ($\geq$ 5 moves in 5 years)	42.7***	20.2
Parent-child separation	11.6***	4.9
New parent figure in household	5.4	5.1
Mean # (std) of above (0-3)	0.65 (0.64)***	0.4(0.7)

[a] The reference period for these risk indicators is birth through age 16. For all other indicators, the reference period is age 9, 11, or 13 through age 16.
$* = p < .05$, $** = p < .01$ $*** = p < .001$
Statistical tests are based on the robust Z-scores for the log-odds ratios estimated in GEE with a logistic link.

TABLE 5. Cluster Means Based on Number of Risks

	Cluster			
	A	B	C	D
	(52.8%)	(14.7%)	(18.9%)	(13.7%)
Risk Category	Mean (std)	Mean (std)	Mean (std)	Mean (std)
Parent Problems	1.1(0.9)	2.1(0.9)	2.7(0.7)	1.0(0.7)
Family Composition	0.6(0.8)	1.6(1.0)	1.8(0.7)	2.3(1.0)
Economic Strains	1.0(0.7)	2.7(0.8)	2.0(0.5)	3.0(0.6)
Quality of Care	0.5(0.9)	0.7(0.8)	1.0(0.6)	2.7(1.0)
Victimization	0.4(0.9)	1.8(0.7)	0.0(0.2)	0.6(0.8)
Instability	0.6(0.9)	2.5(1.0)	1.1(0.8)	1.0(0.6)

Isolated risks. The largest identified cluster of children (Table 5, Group A) included half of all children whose mothers had been involved with the criminal justice system. Although some children classified in this group may have been exposed to different parent or family risks, there were no risks shared by a majority of youth. As a group, these children's parents and other caregivers appear to have had relatively few problems, and there was little indication of economic strain, instability, or inadequate care.

History of abuse. Group B had high economic risks and maternal mental health problems, but the distinguishing characteristic of youth classified in this group was abuse. As shown in Table 6, nearly two-thirds of these youth (64.3 percent) had a history of sexual abuse and more than half (57.8 percent) had been physically abused by a parent.

Pervasive parent problems. Like Group B, high economic risks and maternal mental health problems also characterized Group C, but what distinguished this group was the pervasiveness of parent risks. Not only were maternal mental health problems a prevalent risk factor in this group, but more than 3 out of 4 (77.7 %) of these youth also had a father or other parent figure with mental health problems and 3 out of 5 also had fathers or other parent figures with substance abuse problems (60.3%).

Economic deprivation and single-parent households. A majority of the final group (D) were children living in single-parent households in which there were economic hardships. However, parent problems such as substance abuse and mental illness were minimal among this group.

TABLE 6. Risks Reported for Fifty Percent or More of Youth

Risk	% Within Cluster
Cluster A (Isolated Risks)	
None	
Cluster B (History of Abuse)	
Income below federal poverty level	87.9
Residential instability	85.2
Unemployed caregiver	78.9
Maternal mental illness	68.0
Child sexual abuse	64.3
Single-parent household	63.4
Child physical abuse by parent	57.8
Cluster C (Pervasive Parent Problems)	
Income below federal poverty level	87.8
Maternal mental illness	86.2
Single-parent household	80.1
Parent/Other parent figure mental illness	77.7
Parent/Other parent figure substance abuse	60.3
Unable to meet child's basic needs	50.6
Cluster D (Economic Deprivation and Single-Parent Households)	
Inadequate supervision of child	94.3
Income below federal poverty level	93.6
Unable to meet child's basic needs	81.8
Unemployment	75.4
Single-parent household	71.8

CONCLUSIONS

This article used data from an epidemiologic study of youth in pre-dominantly rural counties in North Carolina to explore differences among children whose mothers had been involved with the criminal justice system. The two key findings from these analyses are that this group is neither a distinct group from children of male offenders nor is it a homogenous group.

First, the majority of youth in the population represented by GSMS whose mothers had been involved with criminal justice authorities also had fathers who had been arrested. Consequently, it is a misnomer to speak of children of female offenders and children of male offenders as if they are two discrete groups. Although the arrest and/or incarceration of mothers and fathers potentially have different immediate and long-term consequences for children, these findings show that a majority of children whose mothers are arrested may be at risk for experiencing not only the consequences associated with maternal arrest, but also those associated with paternal arrest.

Secondly, distinguishable subgroups of youth with meaningfully different parent and family risk profiles were identified. Half of the youth appear to have been in situations that do not seem particularly worrisome. Within this group, one might expect to find occasional children with prevention or intervention needs, but collectively these children generally appear to have had relatively satisfactory and stable family circumstances. The other half is a different story. The other half consisted of children who could be termed "at risk"; however, they were not all traversing the same risk pathway. Some had been abused, others lacked adequate supervision and experienced economic deprivation, and yet others had possibly experienced a multiplicity of risks.

These findings point to the lack of basic information currently available about prevention and intervention programs for children whose mothers become involved in the criminal justice system. For example, which children are these programs reaching? Is it children in the isolated risk group or the at-risk group? Are differences among youth and their families being taken into account in designing programs or are programs using a "one-size-fits-all" approach? What preparation are volunteers and staff receiving to enable them to accurately assess the different needs of children and their families and respond appropriately? Are high risk children being screened for emotional and behavioral problems which may need professional intervention?

Finally, one might choose to take Ockham's razor to these findings and concentrate on addressing the most widespread risks in the backgrounds of these children: economic risks and maternal mental health problems. This raises a different set of questions about the direction of programs for children whose mothers become involved with the criminal justice system, particularly those who serve time.

As correctional populations have grown, there has been a de-emphasis on correctional rehabilitation programs that address education, job preparation, and mental health (Petersilia, 1999), all of which could help to remedy the most pervasive risks that were observed among the children with histories of maternal arrest in the GSMS population. At the same time, there has been an increasing emphasis on programs that address the relationship between parents and their children (i.e., parenting programs, visitation, and so forth). According to a publication by the National Institute of Corrections (NIC, 2002), "for inmates . . . family programs and services can . . . address the forces underlying an inter-generational cycle of crime" (p. 1). It goes on to talk about the "stress, trauma, stigmatization and separation problems for children" associated with parental arrest and confinement. There is no argument that children's emotional reactions to parental arrest and detention are important concerns. But, the results reported here raise the question of whether it is realistic to expect the family programs being implemented in correctional settings to significantly impact intergenerational incarceration without also attacking key issues of poverty and maternal mental health. These are both well-established predictors of the types of serious youth problems that can lead to young people becoming involved in the criminal justice system.

Ultimately, as programs for children affected by parental involvement with the criminal justice system continue to evolve, it will be important for program developers to identify the particular needs of the different subpopulations of youth in their specific service area. Armed with that information, programs will be in a better position to set eligibility criteria, anticipate the demand for services, select assessment tools, and develop means to assure that children and families receive the services they need that the program may not provide. This will mean working across disciplines and service sectors to identify or develop efficacious treatment and prevention strategies for parental substance abuse and mental illness, physical and sexual abuse, and poverty as well as for the emotional and behavioral problems children may experience as a result of those problems. It also means finding ways of delivering the particular mix of services that a particular family may need.

Limitations. The analyses described in this article explored the heterogeniety among a particular group of children whose mothers were arrested as adults. These arrests may or may not have occurred during the children's lifetimes. Clearly, these results are not the final word on the risk profiles of youth whose parents are involved in the criminal justice system. The purpose of these analyses was simply to see if there were discernable and meaningful differences among these youth. Had the sample been defined differently (e.g., only children whose mothers were convicted of a crime, only those whose mothers were detained, only those whose mothers were arrested when they were infants, and so forth), different results may have been obtained. Individuals planning services should determine the specific needs of the populations they are targeting as these findings may not generalize.

Furthermore, these analyses examined risks related to only one of several possible developmental trajectories that may operate in the lifes of children whose parents become involved with criminal authorities–their family situations. Other potentially relevant risk pathways, each with different implications for prevention and intervention, include genetic vulnerability for substance abuse or mental illness, direct effects of low and high magnitude psychological trauma (e.g., witnessing domestic, criminal victimization, parent-child separation), and community context (e.g., influence of delinquent peers, availability of drugs). Examining these other pathways could provide additional information about the heterogeneous needs of these young people and its implications for program planning efforts.

Finally, most of the family risks that were observed in this study were present when children were between the ages of 9 and 16. Because parents' complete criminal justice history cannot be determined from the self-report data used in these analyses, there is no way to know how the observed risks were temporally related to parents' involvement with criminal authorities over time. Consequently, these findings may reflect circumstances that are temporally distant from the index episode of arrest.

REFERENCES

Abram, K. M., Teplin, L. A., & McClelland, G. M. (2003). Comorbidity of severe psychiatric disorders and substance use disorders among women in jail. *American Journal of Psychiatry, 160*, 1007-1010.

Achenbach, T. M., & Edelbrock, C. S. (1981). Behavioral problems and competencies reported by parents of normal and disturbed children aged four through sixteen. *Monographs in Social Research and Child Development, 8*, 1-82.

Allard, P. (2002). *Life sentences: Denying welfare benefits to women convicted of drug offenses.* Washington, DC: The Sentencing Project.

Ammerman, R., Kolko, D., Kirisci, L., Blackson, T., & Dawes, M. (1999). Child abuse potential in parents with histories of substance use disorder. *Child Abuse & Neglect, 23*, 1225-1238.

Angold, A., Prendergast, M., Cox, A., Harrington, R., Simonoff, E., & Rutter, M. L. (1995). The Child and Adolescent Psychiatric Assessment (CAPA). *Psychological Medicine, 25*, 739-53.

Beckerman, A. (1998). Charting a course: Meeting the challenge of permanency planning for children with incarcerated mothers. *Child Welfare, 77*, 513-529.

Bernstein, N. (2005). *All alone in the world.* New York: New Press.

Bloom, B., & Steinhart, D. (1993). *Why punish the children: A reappraisal of the children of incarcerated mothers in America.* San Francisco: National Council on Crime and Delinquency.

Dush-Baskette, S., & Patino, V. (2004). *The National Council on Crime and Delinquency's evaluation of the project development of National Institute of Correction's/ Child Welfare League of America's planning and intervention sites funded to address needs of children of incarcerated parents.* Oakland: CA: National Council on Crime and Delinquency.

Calinski & Harabasz, 1974–cited in text, need reference.

Carlson, J. R. (2001). Prison nursery 2000: A five-year review of the prison nursery at the Nebraska Correctional Center for Women. *Journal of Offender Rehabilitation, 33,* 75-98.

Costello, E. J., Angold, A., Burns, B. J., Stangl D., Erkanli, A., & Wortham, C. M. (1996). The Great Smoky Mountains Study of Youth: goals, designs, methods, and the prevalence of DSM-III-R disorders. *Archive of General Psychiatry, 53,* 1129-36.

Costello, E. J., Farmer E. M., Angold A., Burns, B. J., & Erkanli A. (1997). Psychiatric disorders among American Indian and white youth in Appalachia: The Great Smoky Mountains Study. *American Journal of Public Health, 87,* 827-932.

Costello, E. J., Angold, A., March, J., & Fairbank, J. A. (1998). Life events and post-traumatic stress: the development of a new measure for children and adolescents. *Psychological Medicine, 28,* 1275-88.

Dickon, C. (2005). Family Ties, Through Prison Walls. Retrieved on Feb 18, 2006 http://www.connectforkids.org/articles/family_through_prison.

Giancola, P. R. (2000). Temperament and antisocial behavior in preadolescent boys with or without a family history of a substance use disorder. *Psychology of Addictive Behaviors, 14,* 56-68.

Glueck, S., & Glueck, E. (1950). *Unraveling juvenile delinquency.* Cambridge, MA: Harvard University Press.

Johnston, D. (1995). Effects of parental incarceration. In K. Gabel & D. Johnston (Eds.), *Children of incarcerated parents* (pp. 59-88). New York: Lexington Books.

Johnston, D. (2003). What works: Children of incarcerated offenders. In V. Gadsen (Ed.), *Heading home: Offender reintegration into the family* (pp. 123-154). Landam MD: American Correctional Association.

Johnston, D., & Carlin, M. (1996). Enduring trauma in children of criminal offenders. *Progress: Family Systems Research and Therapy, 6,* 23-39.

Johnston, D., & Gabel, K. (1995). Jailed mothers. In K. Gabel & D. Johnston (Eds.), *Children of incarcerated parents* (pp. 41-56). NY: Free Press.

Kazura, K., & Toth, K. (2004). Playrooms in prison: Helping offenders connect with their children. *Corrections Today, 66,* 128-132.

Keller, T. E., Catalono, R. F., Haggerty, K. P., & Fleming, C. G. (2002). Parent figure transition and delinquency and drug use among early adolescent children of substance abusers. *American Journal of Drug and Alcohol Abuse, 28,* 399-427.

Kleinbaum, D. G., Kupper, L. L., & Morgenstern, H. (1982). *Epidemiology research: Principles and quantitative methods.* New York: Van Nostrand Reinhold.

Koban, L. (1983). Parents in prison: A comparative analysis of the effects of incarceration on the families of men and women. *Research in Law, Deviance and Social Control, 5,* 171-183.

Kupersmidt, J. B., Griesler, P. C., DeRosier, M. E., Patterson, C. J., & Davis, P. W. (1995). Childhood aggression and peer relations in the context of family and neighborhood factors. *Child Development, 66*, 360-375.

Loukas, A., Fitzgerald, H. E., Zucker, R. A., & Eye, A. V. (2001). Parental alcoholism and co-occurring antisocial behavior: Prospective relationships to externalizing behavior problems in their young sons. *Journal of Abnormal Child Psychology, 29*, 91-106.

McCord, J., & McCord, W. (1958). The effects of parental role model of criminality. *Journal of Social Issues, 14*, 66-75.

Mullen, F. (1995). *A tangled web: Public benefits, grandparents, and grandchildren*. Washington, DC: American Association of Retired Persons.

Murray, J., & Farrington, D. P. (2005). Parental imprisonment: Effect on boys' antisocial behaviour and delinquency through the life-course. *Journal of Child Psychology and Psychiatry, 10*, 1-10.

Mustin, J., D'Arville, D., & Scmaltz-Reidt, Y. (Eds.) (2005). *Serving children and families of adult offenders: A directory of programs* (NIC-020200). Washington, D.C.: U. S. Department of Justice, National Institute of Corrections.

National Institute of Corrections (2002). *Special issues in corrections: Services for families of prison inmates*. Longmont, CO: U.S. Department of Justice, National Institute of Corrections.

Petersilia, J. (1999). Parole and prisoner reentry in the United States. In Michael Tonry and Joan Petersilia (eds.), *Prisons*. Chicago: University of Chicago Press.

Phillips, S., & Bloom, B. (1998). In whose best interest? The impact of changing public policy on relatives caring for children with incarcerated parents. *Child Welfare, 77*, 531-541.

Phillips, S. D., Burns, B. J, Wagner, H. R., Kramer, T. L., & Robbins, J. M. (2002). Parental incarceration among youth receiving mental health services. *Journal of Child and Family Studies, 11*, 385-399.

Phillips, S. D., Burns, B. J., Wagner, H. R., & Barth, R. P. (2004). Parental arrest and children in child welfare services agencies. *American Journal of Orthopsychiatry, 2*, 174-186.

Poehlmann, J. (2005). Incarcerated mothers' contact with children. Perceived family relationships, and depressive symptoms. *Journal of Family Psychology, 19*(3), 350-357.

Ross, T., Khashu, A., & Wamsley, M. (2004). *Hard data on hard times: An empirical analysis of maternal incarceration, visitation, and foster care*. New York, Vera Institute.

Sarle, W. S. (1983), *Cubic clustering criterion, SAS Technical Report A-108*. Cary, NC: SAS Institute Inc.

Sharp, S. F. (2004). *Oklahoma study of incarcerated mothers and their children*. University of Oklahoma: Department of Sociology.

Slavin, P. (2004). Mentoring the children of prisoners. *Children's Voices*, September/October.

Smith, A., Krisman, K., Strozler, A. L., & Marley, M. A. (2004). Breaking through the bars: Exploring the experiences of addicted incarcerated parents whose children are cared for by relatives. *Families in Society, 85*, 187-195.

Smith, B. E., & Elstein, S. G. (1994). *Children on hold: Improving the response to children whose parents are arrested and incarcerated.* Washington DC: American Bar Association Center on Children and the Law.

Snyder, Z. K., Carol, T. A., & Coats Mullins, M. M. (2001). Parenting from prison: An examination of a children's visitation program at a women's correctional facility. *Marriage & Family Review, 32,* 33-62.

Stanton, A. (1980). *When mothers go to jail.* Lexington, MA: Lexington Books.

doi:10.1300/J012v17n02_04

Predictors of Loneliness Among Court-Involved and Substance Abusing Mothers

Elizabeth Lehr Essex
Donna Petras
Carol Rippey Massat

SUMMARY. This study examined predictors of loneliness among 94 urban mothers with a history of substance abuse and criminal justice involvement. The study replicated the finding that loneliness is significantly related to level of substance abuse. Significant predictors of loneliness included co-occurring conditions of the mother, the number of minors in the home, the level of domestic violence, informal social support, and service satisfaction. Based on these findings, the authors suggest that

Elizabeth Lehr Essex, PhD, is Assistant Professor, Department of Social Work, College of Health Professions, Governors State University, 1 University Parkway, University Park, IL 60466 (E-mail: e-essex@govst.edu). Donna Petras, PhD, is Assistant Professor and Carol Rippey Massat, PhD, is Associate Professor, Jane Addams College of Social Work, University of Illinois at Chicago, 1040 W. Harrison St., Chicago, IL 60607 (E-mail: dpetras@uic.edu; cmassat@uic.edu).

Support for this research was provided by grants from the National Institute on Drug Abuse (RO1 2520944) and the Jane Addams College of Social Work at the University of Illinois at Chicago. The authors thank Arthur Lurigio and James Swartz for their helpful consultation and their Research Assistants Marvin Lindsey, Stephanie Rice, Lisa Couser, and Adam Turry.

[Haworth co-indexing entry note]: "Predictors of Loneliness Among Court-Involved and Substance Abusing Mothers." Essex, Elizabeth Lehr, Donna Petras, and Carol Rippey Massat. Co-published simultaneously in *Women & Criminal Justice* (The Haworth Press, Inc.) Vol. 17, No. 2/3, 2006, pp. 63-74; and: *Drugs, Women, and Justice: Roles of the Criminal Justice System for Drug-Affected Women* (ed: James A. Swartz, Patricia O'Brien, and Arthur J. Lurigio) The Haworth Press, Inc., 2006, pp. 63-74. Single or multiple copies of this article are available for a fee from The Haworth Document Delivery Service [1-800-HAWORTH, 9:00 a.m. - 5:00 p.m. (EST). E-mail address: docdelivery@haworthpress.com].

doi:10.1300/J012v17n02_05

work with substance abusing mothers involved with the criminal justice system should address multiple ecological levels, including characteristics of the mother and her children, partner relations, and informal and formal social supports. doi:10.1300/J012v17n02_05 *[Article copies available for a fee from The Haworth Document Delivery Service: 1-800-HAWORTH. E-mail address: <docdelivery@haworthpress.com> Website: <http://www.HaworthPress. com> © 2006 by The Haworth Press, Inc. All rights reserved.]*

KEYWORDS. Criminal justice, loneliness, social support, substance abuse, substance abusing mothers, women and criminal justice

INTRODUCTION

Every year more of the women who become involved with the criminal justice system do so because they abuse substances and are involved in a substance use related crime (Greenfeld & Snell, 2000). This is particularly important to society because these women are often mothers who have primary responsibility for caregiving of their children. About 70% of women under correctional sanction are parents, with an average of 2.11 minor children (Greenfield & Snell, 2000). Parental involvement in substance abuse has been shown to be the strongest predictor of child maltreatment (up to 70% of cases; Magura & Laudet, 1996).

Our study examined predictors of loneliness among urban mothers with a history of substance abuse and criminal justice involvement. We came to this topic primarily through our interest in women's parental experiences, and ultimately, their ability to care for and nurture their children. Previous research has found maternal loneliness and social isolation to be associated with child maltreatment, and substance abuse (Coohey, 1996; Farris & Fenaughty, 2002; Miller & Paone, 1998). The conceptual framework underlying our ongoing research is based on the Belsky and Vondra (1989) model of determinants of effective parenting. This model posits multiple, interacting influences on parenting from personal to familial and wider social levels, including (a) parental characteristics; (b) child characteristics; (c) parental partner relations; and (d) parental social networks. Belsky and Vondra (1989) developed their model through intensive examination of the research literature on parenting and based their domains on the research findings regarding aspects of the individual and the environment that had a significant impact on parenting. The model guided us in reviewing past research and organizing specific variable domains for the study on which this article is based. Below, we review elements from the conceptual framework undergirding our focus on loneliness for court-involved substance abusing mothers and our specific hypotheses concerning predictors of loneliness for this population.

ELEMENTS OF THE CONCEPTUAL FRAMEWORK

Loneliness

Conceptually in this study, loneliness is viewed as the subjective experience of feeling socially isolated. Although it may often be related to limited social networks or social support, it is an independent construct (Lubben & Gironda, 2003). For the population of substance abusing mothers who are criminal offenders, loneliness is likely to be of particular importance. First, the experience of loneliness appears to differ by gender. For example, Rokach (2000) in a study of antecedents of loneliness in adulthood, found a main effect for gender across all age groups in individuals' perceptions of the reasons for their loneliness. In a study of alcoholics, Medora and Woodward (1991) found that women alcoholics scored higher on measures of loneliness than did men. Second, previous research has found that social isolation is associated with parenting difficulties and child neglect (Coohey, 1996; Polanski, 1985). Third, loneliness and substance abuse have been positively related in previous studies (James, Johnson, & Raghavan, 2004; Medora & Woodward, 2001; Rokach, 2002). Among older adults, loneliness is a significant risk factor for alcohol abuse relapse (Barrick & Connors, 2002). Fourth, loneliness is a significant factor among the offender population. Rokach and Cripps (1999) found that incarcerated male offenders' loneliness was stigmatized and was influenced by poor childhood attachments.

Parental Characteristics

Given the high incidence of comorbidity of psychopathology and substance abuse (Cochrane et al., 2000), it is significant that previous research has demonstrated a high correlation between loneliness and psychopathology (Peplau, 1985). Laudet, Magura, Vogel, and Knight (2004) found that for persons with co-occurring conditions, loneliness was frequently a relapse trigger. Co-occurring conditions, be they physical, medical or emotional, may limit social contacts in a variety of ways. Physical limitations may reduce one's ability to engage in social activities. Mental or emotional conditions, such as depression, may also reduce one's ability and desire to be with others. In turn, the social isolation may then aggravate depression or other mental illness.

Child Characteristics

Another important influence on loneliness may be the amount of caregiving responsibility that a mother has. Demands of caring for multiple children may reduce one's social contacts (Peplau, 1985). The literature suggests a relationship between the number of children in the home and successful substance abuse treatment and satisfactory socialization (McMahan, Winkel, Suchman, & Luthar, 2002).

Partner Relations

In this study, level of domestic violence was included as an important aspect of partner relations for substance abusing women, who are at increased risk of domestic violence (Davis & DiNitto, 2005). Domestic violence involves relational loss, shame, reduced social networks, and isolation (Farris & Fenaughty, 2002; James, Johnson & Raghaven, 2004). Hendy, Eggen, Gustitus, McLeod, and Ng (2003) found that women in violent relationships who decided to stay in those relationships had a significantly greater fear of loneliness than those who decided to leave the abusive situation.

Social Network Support

Loneliness is negatively associated with social supports for mothers (Gaudin, Polansky, Kilpatrick, & Shilton, 1993). Substance abusing women tend to have weak social support networks and few friends (Miller & Paone, 1998; Schilit & Lisansky-Gomberg, 1987). Among substance abusing persons, spending time with drug-using friends is not sufficient to assuage the sense of loneliness (Reichmann, Kaplan, & Jannson, 2001). Rokach (2002) found that among young adult drug users unfulfilling intimate relationships, significant separations, and social marginality were all significant predictors of loneliness.

Informal social support missing from parents' natural social networks may be provided by formal social service interventions (DePanfilis, 1996). Thus, satisfaction with formal supports may be important in relieving potential loneliness issues of substance abusing court-involved mothers.

METHODS

Research Question

The primary research question addressed was: What predicts loneliness for substance abusing, court-involved mothers? Hypothesized predictors of loneliness included (a) parental characteristics, defined as co-occurring conditions; (b) child characteristics, defined in this study as number of minors in the home; (c) partner relations, defined as the degree of domestic violence experienced by the mother; and (d) social network support, defined as informal social support and satisfaction with substance abuse services. Specifically, we hypothesized that having one or more co-occurring condition, the number of minors in the home, and the degree of domestic violence would have a positive relationship to loneliness, while informal social support and satisfaction with substance abuse services would be negatively related to loneliness.

In addition, we report the relationship between loneliness and the level of substance abuse of the women in our study. Although this was not the primary focus of this study, we believe it is relevant in understanding the importance of loneliness for the women we studied.

Sample

The data from two cross-sectional exploratory studies of substance abusing, court-involved mothers were pooled for our analyses. Nineteen subjects were interviewed in 2000 and 81 subjects were interviewed from 2004-2005. It was deemed acceptable to combine the two data sets as they included the same measures and the samples were drawn from the same population, with the exception of eligibility requirements related to the age of at least one child. Recruitment criteria in 2000 required that at least one coresident child be between the ages of two and eight. In 2004-05, the upper age range was extended, so that all women lived with at least one child between the ages of two and twelve.

To be eligible for the study, women had to be 18 years of age or older, to speak English, and to have had involvement with the criminal justice system and a history of substance abuse. Participants must have received substance abuse services for at least three months. Additionally, subjects had to live with one or more of their own children between the ages of two and twelve.

Potential subjects were referred to the researchers by the Chicago metropolitan area offices of Treatment Alternatives for Safe Communities (TASC). Adults who are substance involved and have been convicted of a criminal offense may be ordered to TASC in lieu of serving a prison sentence. Flyers and letters describing the study were given to TASC, and TASC distributed the information to women who met eligibility criteria. In some cases, the researchers presented this same information to groups of TASC clients, who were invited to participate if eligible. Additionally, subjects were recruited through nomination by study participants. Subjects were interviewed at TASC or university offices, or in participants' own home, depending on their preference. The structured interview, conducted by one of the lead investigators or a trained research assistant, took approximately 1 ½ hours to complete.

Of the 100 women in the pooled 2000 and 2004-05 samples, six were omitted from the present study because of missing data on key study variables, yielding a sample of 94. This sample included 17 subjects recruited in 2000 and 77 recruited in 2004-05. The 17 subjects recruited earlier did not differ from those recruited later on any of the variables in the analyses reported here. Demographically, the only significant difference was that those recruited earlier were younger (means = 31.82 and 36.16 respectively, t [92] = –2.63, p = .01).

The mean age of the 94 women was 35.4 years (SD = 6.3), with an age range from 19 to 50. They were predominantly African American (90.4%), with a small number Latina (4.3%) or non-Hispanic White (5.3%). Only 14.9% were living with a spouse or other partner. Most (75.5%) identified their religious faith as Protestant. Over half (52.1%) did not have a high school degree or GED; the mean years of education was 11.1 (SD = 1.7), with a range of 5-16 years. The income level was very low, with a median income of only $5,000-$9,999. Eighty-three percent of the subjects were unemployed. Subjects lived with a mean of 3.8 other household members (SD = 2.1).

Only 15 subjects reported that their most recent involvement with the criminal justice system was the result of their first arrest. Of the remaining 79 subjects, 50% reported more than six arrests with 25% reporting 20 or more arrests. The charges associated with the subjects' most recent arrest were most often drug possession (39%) and economic crimes (45%), including retail theft, forgery, burglary, prostitution, and drug trafficking. Most of the respondents viewed their main substance abuse problem to be use of heroin (66%) or cocaine (22%).

Variable Domains and Measures

Loneliness was measured by the Revised UCLA Loneliness Scale (Russell, Peplau, & Cutrona, 1980). This widely-used measure includes

20 items rated on a four-point scale (from 1 = *never* to 4 = *often*); 10 items are reverse coded before summing the items, with higher scores indicating higher loneliness. Examples of items include "I lack companionship"; "There is no one I can turn to"; and "I feel left out." Alpha reliability for the study sample was .89.

Level of substance abuse was measured by the drug composite score formed from the Addiction Severity Index (ASI, McLellan, 1985; McGahan, Griffith, Parente, & McLellan, 1986). The drug composite score is formed by an algorithm applied to 13 items pertaining to drug use in the alcohol/drug section of the ASI. We did not include the alcohol composite measure in this study, because alcohol use was reported as a difficulty by only a small minority of the sample (4.4%).

The parental characteristic of *co-occurring conditions* was based on three questions asking whether any member(s) of the household, including the subject, had a chronic illness, disability, or took medication regularly. The formed variable was coded 1 if the subject reported that she had an illness, disability, and or took medication regularly and 0 otherwise.

The child characteristic included in our analyses was the *number of minors in the home*. This was measured by a count of the individuals under age 18 who the subject reported were living in her home.

Partner relations included in our study was defined as degree of *domestic violence* as measured by the Conflict Tactics Scale (18-item version; Straus, 1979). The respondent was asked to rate how often her current or most recent intimate partner used each of 18 violent tactics (e.g., "Smashed, kicked or hit"); the rating scale ranged from 0 = *never* to 6 = *more than 20 times in the past year* [or the last year of the most recent relationship]. Alpha reliability for our sample was .96.

Parental social network support in this study included both informal and formal support. *Informal social support* was measured by the Maternal Social Support Index (Pascoe, Loda, Jeffries, & Earp, 1981). The MSSI items were designed to measure subjective and objective aspects of affective and instrumental social support related both to parenting and in general. Responses to 21 questions, which use a variety of rating scales, were combined into seven items according to an algorithm provided by Pascoe et al. (1981). Alpha reliability for our sample, based on the seven items, was .48.

Formal support was defined as *satisfaction with services*, as measured by the Outpatient Satisfaction Questionnaire (Davis & Hobbs, 1989). The original measure includes three subscales gauging access to service, the physical environment for service provision, and the quality of the care received. Items are rated on a four point scale from 1 = *very dissatisfied/no definitely not* to 4 = *very satisfied/yes, definitely.* Respondents answered the questions in reference to their current or most recent substance abuse service provider. For this study, the sum of the items from the physical environment (3 items) and care (12 items) subscales were used, since many of the items in the access subscale (e.g., directions for parking) were not applicable to the full sample. Alpha reliability for the 15 item scale used in out study was .93.

Table 1 reports descriptive findings for these measures as used in our study.

FINDINGS

Loneliness and Substance Abuse

A Pearson correlation was conducted to determine the bivariate relationship between loneliness and substance abuse. There was a moderate significant relationship between loneliness and the ASI drug composite scores: $r = .25$, $p = .01$. It should be noted that most respondents reported low use on the 11 ASI items asking for the number of days of

TABLE 1. Descriptives of Study Measures

Measure	Study Sample ($N = 94$)
Revised UCLA Loneliness Scale (Range = 20 to 80)	Mean = 39.3 (SD = 11.4) Range = 21 to 69
ASI Drug Composite (Range = 0 to 1)	Mean = .11 (SD = .07) Range = 0 to .40
Co-occurring Conditions (1 = yes, 0 = no)	1 = 37%
Number of Minors	Mean = 2.6 (SD = 1.5) Range = 1 to 7
Conflict Tactics Scale (Range = 0 to 108)	Mean = 7.9 (SD = 15.8) Range = 0 to 105
Maternal Social Support Index (Range = 0 to 19)	Mean = 10.7 (SD = 3.2) Range = 2 to 17
Outpatient Satisfaction Questionnaire (Range = 15 to 60)	Mean = 53.3 (SD = 7.3) Range = 35 to 60

drug use within the past month, possibly due to the fact that almost all were currently receiving substance abuse treatment. Hence, the truncated variability in the drug composite scores may have lowered the magnitude of the correlation.

Predictors of Loneliness

To test our hypothesis concerning predictors of loneliness, we conducted an ordinary least squares regression, regressing the loneliness variable on the variables hypothesized as predictors. Due to the small sample size, we did not include demographic control variables (e.g., age, education, and income). In addition, preliminary analyses conducted prior to those reported here suggested demographic control variables did not change the regression results.

Table 2 displays the results of the regression analysis. All relationships were significant and in the hypothesized direction. Having a co-occurring condition, a greater number of minor children in the home, and experiencing a higher level of domestic violence were positively related to loneliness. The two kinds of social network support variables, informal social support and satisfaction with services, were negatively related to loneliness. The level of informal social support had the strongest relationship to loneliness, with the largest standardized beta and probability level. The total model accounted for 40 percent of the variance in subjects' loneliness.

TABLE 2. Summary of Ordinary Least Squares Regression Analysis for Variables Predictive of Loneliness[a]

Variable	*B*	*SE B*	β
Co-occurring conditions	5.91**	1.98	.25
Number of minors	1.35*	.65	.18
Domestic violence	.17**	.06	.24
Informal social support	−1.40***	.31	−.40
Service satisfaction	−.31*	.13	−.20
R^2		.40	

[a]$N = 94$.

*$p < .05$. **$p < .01$. ***$p < .001$.

DISCUSSION

Our research was based on an ecological model, linking the personal experiences of court and substance-involved mothers to multiple levels of the personal and social environment. Based on our conceptual framework, we posited and found support for viewing loneliness in this population as stemming, at least in part, from: (a) characteristics of the women themselves (the presence or absence of co-occurring conditions; (b) child characteristics (number of minors in the home); (c) partner relations (degree of domestic violence experienced in their relations with partners); and (d) informal and formal social supports. Our particular interest in loneliness emanated from a body of research suggesting loneliness is a risk factor for difficulties in parenting. For the women in our study, loneliness was also related to increased substance abuse. Thus, considering ways to reduce loneliness may impact severity of substance abuse as well as the parenting experiences of this population. Service providers working with this group should be prepared to assess and address multiple domains, including consideration of co-occurring conditions, family circumstances, and social supports. One possible cause for optimism is our finding that mothers' satisfaction with substance abuse services was a negative predictor of loneliness. This supports literature suggesting that effective provision of formal services may provide a substitute for weak or dysfunctional social support networks.

A number of limitations qualify the interpretation of findings from this exploratory study. Because the population is hard to reach, the authors used a nonprobability sampling method. As a result, the study results may not be generalizable to the larger population of substance abusing, court-involved mothers. Limitations related to the measures included the relatively low scores and variability on the ASI drug composite and the low reliability of the Maternal Social Support Index. Further, measures available in our data set restricted the number and kinds of variables we could include from each of the domains of our theoretical framework. Finally, in light of the cross-sectional nature of our analyses and small sample size, any specification of relationships between variables in our study must be very tentative. For example, although we modeled loneliness as a dependent variable, the relationship between loneliness and one or more of our hypothesized predictors may in fact be reciprocal or in the reverse direction.

We hope our exploratory study is an impetus for further quantitative and qualitative research. Future longitudinal studies with larger samples and additional variables (e.g., parenting behavior) could lead to greater understanding of relationships between loneliness and other constructs identified in our study. In-depth qualitative research may also help illuminate the pathways related to loneliness and their implications for women offenders and their children.

REFERENCES

Barrick, C., & Connors, G. J. (2002). Relapse prevention and maintaining abstinence in older adults with alcohol use disorders. *Drugs & Aging, 19,* 583-594.

Belsky, J., & Vondra, J. (1989). Lessons from child abuse: The determinants of parenting. In D. Cicchetti and V. Carlson (Eds.), *Child maltreatment* (pp. 153-202). Cambridge, UK: Cambridge University Press.

Cochrane, J., Goering, P. Durbin, J., Butterill, D., Dumas, J. & Wasylenki, D. (2000). Tertiary mental health services: II. Subpopulations and best practices for service delivery. *Canadian Journal of Psychiatry, 45,* 185-191.

Coohey, C. (1996). Child maltreatment: Testing the social isolation hypothesis. *Child Abuse & Neglect, 20*(3), 241-254.

Davis, D., & Hobbs, G. (1989). Measuring outpatient satisfaction with rehabilitation services. *Quality Review Bulletin, 15,* 192-197.

Davis, D. R., & DiNitto, D. M. (2005). Gender and the use of drugs and alcohol: Fact, fiction, and unanswered questions. In C. A. McNeece, & D. M. DiNitto (Eds.), *Chemical dependency: A systems approach* (3rd ed.). Boston Allyn: & Bacon.

DePanfilis, D. (1996). Social isolation of neglectful families: A review of social support assessment and intervention models. *Child Maltreatment: Journal of the American Professional Society on the Abuse of Children, 1,* 37-52.

Farris, C. A., & Fenaughty, A. M. (2002). Social isolation and domestic violence among female drug users. *American Journal of Drug and Alcohol Abuse, 28,* 339-351.

Gaudin, J. M., Polansky, N. A. Kilpatrick, A. C., & Shilton, P, (1993) Loneliness, depression, stress, and social supports in neglectful families. *American Journal of Orthopsychiatry, 63*(4), 597-605.

Greenfeld, L. A., & Snell, T. L. (2000). *Women Offenders.* Washington, DC: Bureau of Justice Statistics, U.S. Department of Justice.

Hendy, H. M., Eggen, D., Gustitus, C., McLeod, K. C., & Ng, P. (2003). Decision to leave scale: Perceived reasons to stay in or leave violent relationships. *Psychology of Women Quarterly, 27,* 162-173.

James, S. E., Johnson, J., & Raghaven, C. (2004). "I couldn't go anywhere": Contextualizing violence and drug abuse: A social network study. *Violence against women, 10,* 991-1014.

Laudet, A. B., Magura, S., Vogel, H. S., & Knight, E. L. (2004). Perceived reasons for substance misuse among persons with a psychiatric disorder. *American Journal of Orthopsychiatry, 74,* 365-375.

Lubben, J. E., & Gironda, M. W, (2003) Centrality of social ties to the health and well-being of older adults. In B. Berkman & L. Harootyan (Eds.), *Social work and health care in an aging society* (pp. 319-350). New York: Springer.

Magura, S., & Laudet, A. B. (1996). Parental substance abuse and child maltreatment: Review and implications for intervention. *Children and Youth Services Review, 18*, 193-220.

McGahan, P. L., Griffith, J. A., Parent, R., & McLellan, A. T. (1986). *Addiction Severity Index composite scores manual.* Philadelphia: Treatment Research Institute.

McLellan, A. T. (1985). New data from the Addiction Severity Index: Reliability and validity in three centers. *Journal of Nervous and Mental Disorders, 173*, 412-423.

McMahan, T. J., Winkel, J. D., Suchman, N. E., & Luthar, S. S. (2002). Drug dependence, parenting responsibilities, and treatment history: Why doesn't mom go for help? *Drug and Alcohol Dependence. 6*, 105-114.

Medora, N. P., & Woodward, J. C. (1991). Factors associated with loneliness among alcoholics in rehabilitation centers. *The Journal of Social Psychology, 131*, 769-779.

Miller, M., & Paone, D. (1998). Social network characteristics as mediators in the relationship between sexual abuse and HIV risk. *Social Science and Medicine, 47*, 765-777.

Pascoe, J. M., Loda, F. A., Jeffries, V., & Earp, J. A. (1981). The association between mothers' social support and provision of stimulation to their children. *Developmental and Behavioral Pediatrics, 2*, 15-19.

Peplau, L. A. (1985). Loneliness research: Basic concepts and findings. In I. G. Sarason. & B. R. Sarason (Eds.), *Social support: Theory, research, and applications* (pp. 269-286). Durdrecht: Martinus Nijhoff.

Polanski, N. A. (1985). Determinants of loneliness among neglectful and other low-income mothers. *Journal of Social Service Research, 8*, 1-15.

Reichmann, S., Kaplan, C. D., & Jannson, I. (2001). Social epidemiologic comparisons in a European cohort of substance-dependent therapeutic community clients: A case-oriented analysis. *International Journal of Social Welfare, 10*, 224-234.

Rokach, A. (2000). Perceived causes of loneliness in adulthood. *Journal of Social Behavior and Personality, 15*, 67-84.

Rokach, A. (2002). Determinants of loneliness of young adult drug users. *The Journal of Psychology, 13*, 613-630.

Rokach, A., & Cripps, J. E. (1999). Incarcerated men and the perceived sources of their loneliness. *International Journal of Offender Therapy and Comparative Criminology, 43*, 78-89.

Russell, D., Peplau, L. A., & Cutrona, C. E. (1980). The revised UCLA Loneliness Scale: Concurrent and discriminant validity evidence. *Journal of Personality and Social Psychology, 39*, 472-480.

Schilit, R., & Lisansky-Gomberg, E. (1987). Social support structures of women in treatment for alcoholism. *Health & Social Work, 12*, 187-195.

Straus, M. A. (1979). Measuring intrafamily conflict and violence: The conflict tactics (CT) scales. *Journal of Marriage and the Family, 41*, 75-88.

doi:10.1300/J012v17n02_05

Beyond Gender Responsivity: Considering Differences Among Community Dwelling Women Involved in the Criminal Justice System and Those Involved in Treatment

Sheryl Pimlott Kubiak

Cynthia L. Arfken

SUMMARY. As the debate regarding gender responsive strategies continues, there is little attention to differences that exist *within* gender. Attention to within gender differences is of particular importance in community contexts where many women involved in the criminal justice (CJ) system are located and receiving treatment with non-CJ involved women. Using a national data set we found 43.6% of the CJ women had 4

Sheryl Pimlott Kubiak, PhD, MSW, is Assistant Professor in the College of Social Science at Michigan State University. Cynthia L. Arfken, PhD, is Associate Professor in the Department of Psychiatry and Behavioral Neurosciences at Wayne State University.

Address correspondence to: Sheryl Pimlott Kubiak, PhD, College of Social Science, Michigan State University, 254 Baker Hall, East Lansing, MI 48224.

[Haworth co-indexing entry note]: "Beyond Gender Responsivity: Considering Differences Among Community Dwelling Women Involved in the Criminal Justice System and Those Involved in Treatment." Kubiak, Sheryl Pimlott, and Cynthia L. Arfken. Co-published simultaneously in *Women & Criminal Justice* (The Haworth Press, Inc.) Vol. 17, No. 2/3, 2006, pp. 75-94; and: *Drugs, Women, and Justice: Roles of the Criminal Justice System for Drug-Affected Women* (ed: James A. Swartz, Patricia O'Brien, and Arthur J. Lurigio) The Haworth Press, Inc., 2006, pp. 75-94. Single or multiple copies of this article are available for a fee from The Haworth Document Delivery Service [1-800-HAWORTH, 9:00 a.m. - 5:00 p.m. (EST). E-mail address: docdelivery@haworthpress.com].

or more areas of need compared with 16.5% of non-CJ women currently in treatment. Implications for training of treatment professionals and supervising agents, as well as the need for service expansion that prevents probation/parole failures are discussed. doi:10.1300/J012v17n02_06

[Article copies available for a fee from The Haworth Document Delivery Service: 1-800-HAWORTH. E-mail address: <docdelivery@haworthpress.com> Website: <http://www.HaworthPress.com> © *2006 by The Haworth Press, Inc. All rights reserved.]*

KEYWORDS. Treatment, probation, parole, mental health, substance abuse

INTRODUCTION

Deeply rooted in feminist ideology are tensions between theories that exaggerate and those that minimize differences between females and males. Feminist theories that exaggerate female-male differences often essentialize women, positing women as "other" to a male norm, whereas theories that minimize differences imply symmetry and equivalence within gender, often obscuring discrepancies in power and social value. The tension between these theoretical constructs often has real world implications that demand more complicated solutions than this dichotomy allows (Hare-Mustin & Marecek, 1998).

One such 'real world' implication involves the classification and treatment of women involved in the criminal justice system. Ongoing discussions within the criminal justice literature debate the need for gender responsive strategies in assessment, classification and services that accentuate male and female differences. Some argue that gender responsive strategies exaggerate the differences between males and females (Andrews, Bonta, & Wormith, 2006; Dowden & Andrews, 1999), while others believe that the minority status of women within the criminal justice system coupled with gender differences in offending behavior and risk, support the need for gender specific responses (Belenko, 2006; Bloom, Owen & Covington, 2003, Holfreter & Morash, 2003). Within the criminal justice system–and particularly within institutional settings–this debate has far reaching implications for shaping service delivery.

As the debate continues there has been little attention to the differences that may exist *within* gender–particularly in community contexts. Although "involvement in the criminal justice system" usually invokes images of confinement in jail or prison, the majority of felony-convicted women (85%), are in the community on either probation or parole sentences (Greenfield & Snell, 1999). Often treatment participation is required as a condition of probation or parole and participation. Such mandated participation in community treatment often pairs women in the criminal justice system with other women who have substance abuse or mental health disorders, but no involvement in the criminal justice system. Women in treatment may have more in common with women in the criminal justice system than other women in the community. However, even though these commonalities exist, differences between those in treatment while under criminal justice supervision and those in treatment who are not supervised have implications for service delivery. For instance, women involved in the criminal justice system experience a social stigma associated with conviction that may limit resources and opportunities (Kubiak, 2005). This distinction may or may not be addressed or understood in therapeutic contexts, but we know little about other within gender differences that may be present.

This paper suggests that the emphasis on male/female differences within confined settings may have inadvertently minimized the within gender differences that women involved in the criminal justice system may experience in community treatment settings. Determining these differences will assist community treatment providers, criminal justice supervision personnel and policy makers in understanding *within* gender differences and creating 'situationally responsive' services.

BACKGROUND

The criminal justice system spans a continuum that begins with arrest. Individuals may leave the continuum through charges being dropped or move along the continuum through arraignment, trial, and if convicted, sentencing. A recent study of women convicted of felony drug offenses found that 94% received sentences other than incarceration in the state prison with most sentenced to 36-48 months probation with conditions that included participation in substance abuse and/or mental health treatment (Kubiak, Siefert & Boyd, 2004). A comparison of these women on probation with other low income women in the same community found that the women on probation were more likely to meet symptom criteria for a major depressive disorder, PTSD and alcohol and drug dependence. Similarly, the women on probation were more likely to be homeless and unemployed than the low-income women (Kubiak, Siefert & Boyd, 2004).

Treatment available to women on probation or parole is generally not found exclusively in criminal justice programs but is usually embedded within other community substance abuse and/or mental health programs (Wellish, Prendergast & Anglin, 1994). In fact, over a third (36%) of all admissions into publicly funded substance abuse treatment programs are referred by criminal justice personnel (SAMHSA Treatment Episode Data, 2003). Women entering publicly funded treatment have been found to have more severe problems at assessment when compared to men in the same system (Arfken, Klein, diMenza & Schuster, 2001). For example, women were found to have more severe drug use patterns, lower income, educational and employment levels, were more likely to live with their children and have a spouse that uses illegal drugs (Arfken et al., 2001; Hser, Huang, Teruya & Anglin, 2003).

However, similar to the criminal justice system, treatment systems in the community continue to struggle with gender specific strategies. Gender responsive strategies for women in community based organizations include attention to the etiology of addiction, self-esteem, cultural issues, relationships, interpersonal violence, employment, parenting and childcare, gender discrimination/harassment and attention to grief and loss issues (Center for Substance Abuse Treatment [CSAT], 1994) and mirror strategies suggested for women involved in the criminal justice system by National Institute of Corrections (Bloom, Owen & Covington, 2003), CSAT (1999) and several researchers (O'Brien, 2001; Holtfreter & Morash, 2003).

If suggested treatment strategies are similar, are there differences between groups of women? Comparisons between incarcerated women and epidemiologic samples have concluded that women in prisons and jails are far more likely to experience substance abuse and/or mental health disorders than women in the general population (Jordan, Schlenger, Fairbank & Caddell, 1996; Teplin, Abram, McClelland, 1996). However, these studies were diagnostic in nature and did not consider holistic treatment needs nor make comparisons of women under criminal justice supervision living in the community, or those involved in treatment.

Current Study

The goal of this study is to examine the similarities and differences *within* groups of women, using a nationally representative, community-based sample, to better inform criminal justice and treatment professionals. The focus of this examination is on comparing issues within several life domains that might be indicative of the need for services.

These domains are generally included in psychosocial assessments as well as criminal justice system assessments of recidivism risks and associated service needs. To accomplish this, we examine three mutually exclusive groups of adult women living in the community. These groups are (1) those involved in the criminal justice system, (2) those involved in mental health and substance abuse treatment system but not involved in the criminal justice system and (3) women not associated with either criminal justice or mental health and substance abuse treatment.

METHODS

For this secondary analysis, we used the 2002 National Survey on Drug Use and Health (NSDUH). The NSDUH is a comprehensive national survey of self reported drug use and treatment involvement conducted yearly by the Substance Abuse and Mental Health Services Administration (SAMHSA). It measures the prevalence and correlates of drug use in the U.S. using a multistage area probability sample for each of the 50 states. The sampling frame includes the civilian, non-institutionalized population aged 12 and older. In 2002, there was a response rate of 79% yielding 54,079 records in the public use file. Because of the differences between juvenile and adult criminal justice systems, the analyses are restricted to the 19,444 adult women (age 18 or older) who completed the 2002 NSDUH questionnaire.

Definitions of Groups

1. CJ Group (n = 713): Women were coded as being involved in the criminal justice system if they had a positive response to one or more of the following questions: (1) Not counting minor traffic violations, how many times during the past 12 months have you been arrested and booked for breaking a law; (2) Were you on probation at any time during the past 12 months; (3) Were you on parole, supervised release, or any other conditional release from prison at any time during the past 12 months?
2. Treatment Group (n = 2,035): Women were coded as being involved in mental health and/or substance abuse treatment services (referred to as 'treatment group') if they had a positive responses to one or move of the following questions: (1) During the past 12 months, have you stayed overnight in a hospital or other facility to receive treatment or counseling for any problem you were having with

your emotions, nerves, or mental health (exculding substance abuse); (2) During the past 12 months, did you receive any outpatient treatment or counseling for any problem you were having with your emotions, nerves, or mental health; (3) During the past 12 months have you received any treatment of problems with drug and/or alcohol in either an outpatient clinic, residential facility, mental health facility or acute care hospital.

3. Baseline Group (n = 16,696): Finally, we employ a 'baseline group', consisting of those without treatment or criminal justice involvement, to provide context and comparison in our analysis.

Definition of Service Needs

As noted above, the areas assessed for this study reflect domains associated with routine psychosocial assessments as well as criminal justice inventories of service needs. We were interested in what needs the individual might present to a treatment or criminal justice professional in the commmunity. As an organizing tool we used the domains of a popular criminal justice assessment tool–the Level of Service Inventory–LSI (Andrews & Bonta, 1995) using items in the NSDUH that capture the essence of LSI domains. Although the LSI has been validated in studies that include women, statistically significant differences between men and women emerge on most domains (Holsinger, Lowenkamp & Latessa, 2003) and some argue that it could be more effective in measuring gender specific needs (Van Voorhis, Peiler, Presser, Spiropoulis & Sutherland, 2001). Some slight modifications were made to the LSI domains (e.g., rather than criminal justice history, current criminal activity was used) to reflect a comparison with a non-criminal justice population and the limits of the data. The domains include: (1) current criminal involvement; (2) education/employment; (3) financial; (4) family/marital; (5) accomodations; (6) leisure/recreation; (7) companions; (8) alcohol/drug use; and (9) emotional problems. In each domain we choose variables within the NSDUH that would best reflect service needs. Generally, the LSI is scored using a range of risk levels within each domain that represent the level of corresponding need. In this study, variables within each domain were re-coded to reflect a dictomous scoring (0/1) representing the presence or absence of a particular need. These domains and their content items are described below.

1. Current Criminal Activity. The two items used to assess current criminal activity were: During the past 12 months, (a) how many

times have you sold illegal drugs, and (b) how many times have you stolen or tried to steal anything worth more than $50. The answers were scored as positive if the response was one or greater for each item.

2. Education/Employment. The two items used to assess educational and employent need were: (a) highest educational achievement (scored positively if the woman did not complete high school) and (b) currently not working and wanting to be (scored negatively for women in school, working part time or engaged as full time care-givers).

3. Financial. The two items used to assess financial need were: (a) receipt of any government program subsidy (including Medicaid, food stamps, welfare, reduced lunch program) during the past twelve months, and (b) a family income of $10,000 or less.

4. Family/Marital. The three items used to assess family/marital needs were: (a) presence of dependent children in the home under the age of 18; (b) currently being pregnant, and (c) "How many times during the past 12 months did your partner or spouse hit or threaten to hit you?" We did not include absence of a partner in this domain because of conflicting findings. It is considered a protective factor in the mental health literature (Kessler, Berglund, Demler, Jin, Merikangas, & Waters, 2005) but a risk for women involved in the criminal justice system (Griffin & Armstrong, 2003).

5. Accomodations. The two items used to assess instability of residences were: (a) During the last 5 years how often have you moved? (3 or more was scored as indicative of need), and (b) During the past 12 months how often have you moved? (2 or more was scored as indicative of need).

6. Leisure and Recreation. The two items used to assess lack of, or, inappropriate leisure and recreational hobbies were: (a) How often do you get a kick out of doing dangerous things; and (b) How often do you like to test yourself by doing something risky? Both items were scored positively if the women answered "sometimes" or "always."

7. Companions. The two items used to assess nonsupportive companions were: (a) How many friends do you have that really like or care about you? ("none" was scored postively), and (b) How many of your friends get drunk at least once per week? ("most" or "all" were scored positively).

8. Alcohol or Drug Use. The two items used to assess alcohol or drug use were: (a) In the past year have you used any illegal drug, with

the exception of marijuana? and (b) meeting diagnostic criteria for a subtance abuse or dependency diagnosis, per DSM IV R criteria, (American Psychiatric Association, 2001) for alcohol or drugs.

9. Emotional or Personal Problems. The two items used to assess emotional or personal were: (a) serious mental illness (SMI), and (b) poor or fair self-rated health. SMI is determined using the K-6 (Kessler, Andrews, Colpe, Hiripi, et al., 2002) embedded within the survey. The six items relate to symptoms of psychological distress in the previous 12 months and are scored on a 5-point Likert scale from 0 (none of the time) to 4 (all of the time). The range of summed scores is 0–24 with scores of 13 or above classified as indicating an SMI (Kessler, et al., 2002) and scored positively for our purposes. The self-rated health question asks a person to rate their health on a 5-point scale from excellent to poor. Those who rated their health as fair or poor were scored positively.

Analysis

The three groups were compared on demographics, individual items and domains using proportions and means incorporating the complex sampling design and weighting of responses to the U.S. population. All analyses were conducted using Stata 9 (StataCorp, College Station, TX). A domain was scored positively if a woman scored positively on any item within the domain. The possible number of domains was 9 with the actual range of responses from 0-9. The mean number of domains for the entire population of adult women was 1.5 (95% CI = 1.53, 1.59).

RESULTS

As shown in Table 1, the three groups varied on every demographic characteristics examined (all comparisons using a design-based F statistic were significant at $p < .0001$). Women in the treatment group were predominately white (79.9%) with 33.7% attending some college. Women in the criminal justice system were young (57.6% under 35), disproportionately minority (44.3%) with nearly a third (32.3%) not completing high school.

Examining the demographic characteristics we find that 10.1% of those in the treatment group and 6.1% of the baseline group have a history of arrest (Table 1) demonstrating a potential intersection between groups

TABLE 1. Demographic Characteristics by Group

Demographic	Baseline Group 87.8%	Treatment Group (MH or SA) 10.1%	CJ Group 2.1%
Female	100	100	100
Age			
18-25	13.8	12.6	36.3
26-34	15.7	20.0	21.3
35-49	29.8	37.6	33.1
50+	40.7	29.7	9.4
Race			
White	70.5	79.9	55.7
Black	12.1	7.7	21.2
Hispanic	11.6	6.7	15.8
Asian	3.9	3.7	1.7
Other	1.9	2.0	5.7
Education			
Less than High School	16.9	12.7	32.3
High School Grad	34.0	25.5	38.2
Some College	26.7	28.1	23.9
College Grad or Higher	22.4	33.7	5.7
Criminal Justice Involvement			
Arrest Ever	6.1	10.1	100.0
Arrest in Past Year	0	0	56.2
Current Criminal Justice Supervision	0	0	64.9
Treatment During Past 12 Months			
Mental Health Treatment	0	97.8	21.7
Substance Abuse Treatment	0	4.3	15.9
Symptoms of Depression	18.5	64.2	38.0
Symptoms of Trauma Related Disorder	13.5	44.2	32.9

Note: unweighted sample sizes are 16,696 for no treatment or criminal justice involvement, 2,035 for treatment involvement and 713 for criminal justice involvement. All analyses were conducted with samples weighted and incorporating the complex sample design. All comparisons between the three groups were significant at $p < 0.0001$.

over time. Similarly, the criminal justice group demonstrated an interface with treatment during the past year (21.7% for mental health, 15.9% for substance abuse). Furthermore, 38.0% of women with criminal justice involvement reported depressive symptoms and 32.9% reported symptoms related to traumatic exposure, much higher than the 18.5% and 13.5% (respectively) of the baseline group that reported similar symptoms.

A higher percentage of the CJ group scored positively on 17 of the 19 individual items than women in the other two groups (Table 2). Women in the treatment group scored highest on SMI and physical health items. Women in the baseline group demonstrated lower levels of need than either the treatment or CJ group in all but two areas–those with less than a high school education and the proportion of those who were pregnant.

TABLE 2. Percentage of Adult Women Who Scored Positively on Individual Items by Groups

Domains and Items	Baseline Group 87.8%	Treatment Group (MH or SA) 10.1%	CJ Group 2.1%
Criminal Activity			
Selling drugs past 12 months	0.6	1.8	6.4
Ever stole merchandise worth $50 or more	0.5	0.8	9.7
Education/Employment			
Less than H.S.	16.9	12.7	32.3
Unemployed	5.7	5.2	15.3
Financial			
Received government assistance	13.3	16.2	38.0
Poverty (> $10,000 family income)	8.1	9.7	21.6
Family/Marital			
Partner hits/threatens	2.1	3.1	7.8
Pregnant	2.1	1.0	4.8
Kid under 18	41.7	44.6	58.6
Accommodation			
Moved < 3x in 5 years	12.0	20.3	34.9
Moved < 2x in past year	6.4	10.6	24.9
Leisure/Recreation			
Risk taker	7.8	12.8	20.1
Likes dangerous activities	10.4	16.1	23.8
Companions			
None that 'care'	4.9	6.9	12.0
All drunk at least once per week	3.6	5.5	21.8
Alcohol/Drug Use			
Any illegal drug use (except marijuana)	5.8	12.3	31.5
Substance use disorder	4.6	12.7	31.3
Emotional/Personal Problems			
Serious mental illness	7.2	36.9	25.0
Fair or poor self-rated health	12.7	18.4	17.6

Note: unweighted sample sizes are 16,696 for no treatment or criminal justice involvement, 2,035 for treatment involvement and 713 for criminal justice involvement. All analyses were conducted with samples weighted and incorporating the complex sample design. All comparisons between the three groups were significant at $p < 0.0001$.

Nearly a third (31.5%) of the criminal justice involved women used illegal drugs in the past year (excluding marijuana) with a similar proportion (31.3%) meeting criteria for an alcohol or drug disorder. This proportion was nearly three times that of the treatment group and five times that of the baseline group. Underscoring the omnipresence of alcohol and other drugs in their lives, 21.8% of the CJ women reported that 'most or all' of their friends get drunk at least once per week.

Reflecting these individual need items, the nine domains also demonstrate greater needs for the CJ involved women when compared to the other two groups (Table 3), with the exception of the emotional/personal problems domain. Most striking was that in four domains (education/employment, finance, accommodations and alcohol/drugs) the CJ group was at least 20 percentage points higher than the other two groups in assessed need. In addition, a majority of the CJ group was assessed as needing services within the family/marital domain (61.5%). On average, the CJ group scored positively in 3.44 domains compared to 2.05 for women in the treatment group and 1.46 for women in the baseline group.

In Table 4, the distribution of effected domains is presented. The overwhelming majority of women in the CJ group (96.8%) scored positively

TABLE 3. Percentage of Adult Women Who Score Positive in Each Domain by Group

Domain	Baseline Group 87.8%	Treatment Group 10.1%	CJ Group 2.1%
Criminal activity	0.9	2.3	14.1
Education/employment	21.1	17.3	41.4
Finance	18.3	20.9	46.8
Family/marital	43.2	46.2	61.5
Accommodations	14.5	22.8	43.0
Leisure/recreational	12.9	20.3	28.6
Companions	8.3	11.8	28.9
Alcohol/drugs	8.8	19.1	42.6
Emotional/personal problems	18.1	44.6	36.9
Mean number of domains	1.46	2.05	3.44
(95% confidence intervals)	(1.42, 1.49)	(1.94, 2.16)	(3.20, 3.66)

Note: unweighted sample sizes are 16,696 for no treatment or criminal justice involvement, 2,035 for treatment involvement and 713 for criminal justice involvement. All analyses were conducted with samples weighted and incorporating the complex sample design. All comparisons between the three groups were significant at $p < 0.0001$.

TABLE 4. Distribution of Adult Women Who Scored Positively on Domains by Group

Domain	Baseline 87.8%	Treatment Group 10.1%	CJ Group 2.1%
0-1 Domains	59.0	42.1	13.2
2-3 Domains	33.5	41.2	43.2
4-5 Domains	6.8	14.0	30.8
6-9 Domains	0.6	2.5	12.8

Note: unweighted sample sizes are 16,696 for no treatment or criminal justice involvement, 2,035 for treatment involvement and 713 for criminal justice involvement. All analyses were conducted with samples weighted and incorporating the complex sample design. All comparisons between the three groups were significant at $p < 0.0001$.

in at least one domain with 43.6% scoring positively in four or more of the domains. In contrast, 86.7% of the women in the treatment group and 75.6% of the baseline group experienced at least one effected domain and 16.5% of the treatment and 7.4% of the baseline group scored positively in four or more domains.

DISCUSSION

This study utilized a national data set to examine within gender differences between three groups of community dwelling women; those involved in the criminal justice system, those involved in treatment, and those involved in neither. The assessment of nine life domains, that are of interest to treatment or criminal justice professionals, demonstrated that women in the criminal justice system have multiple areas of need that surpass not only epidemiologic estimates, but also those of women already involved in the treatment system.

The effected domains provide a proxy for service needs and clearly illustrate the complex task a treatment or criminal justice professional would encounter in facilitating treatment delivery. Nearly half of the CJ group had four or more areas of need. This would mean that beyond a need for mental health or substance abuse treatment, a treatment professional may also need to expend time, energy and resources on housing, financial instability and employment concerns.

Our study goes beyond previous studies that identify the complex needs of women in the criminal justice system to explore the real world implications of potentially masking important differences between women within community settings. We found that women involved in the criminal justice system vary significantly in both demographic characteristics and level of need from women in the general population as well as those involved in substance abuse and mental health treatment. These within gender differences are of particular importance for criminal justice and treatment professionals responsible for facilitating behavioral changes and monitoring treatment compliance. In addition, this information will assist policy makers in understanding the variation of need that exists–even within gender specific programming. More specifically, this comparison argues the need for more specialized services for women involved in the criminal justice system, rather than treatment as usual.

Gender Responsive Treatment

Advocates of gender responsive treatment for women involved in the criminal justice system have suggested that women may be more appropriately treated within the community. "An advantage of using community corrections for women who do not pose any risk to public safety is that existing services often can meet many needs, for example adult education programs, job readiness programs, and community mental health services" (Holtfreter & Morash, 2003, p. 153). However, existing community services–even services that provide gender specific services–may not be equipped to understand and address the complexity of need that women within the criminal justice system present with. In addition treatment professionals within these community service agencies may not understand how the criminal justice system operates or the stigma associated with being convicted."

Complexity of Need

Nearly half (43.6%) of the women with criminal justice system involvement had four or more areas of their life that required supportive services. Many of the identified areas of need have also been labeled criminogenic needs–or those most closely associated with recidivism (Andrews & Bonta, 2003). A recent study of the needs of women involved in the criminal justice system found that those at highest risk for recidivism were those with substance abuse, mental health, employment and child related needs (Holfreter & Morash, 2003). The authors of that study suggest that holistic programs or those that provide wrap around services that facilitate access to numerous service providers would be helpful for those demonstrating higher levels of risk. However, holistic or wrap around services that address multiple needs are rare even though supervising agents who refer to community based agencies may assume their existence. Although case management services–in which one person is coordinating service delivery–would certainly be an asset, many assume that the supervising agent is performing this function. Although probation and parole officers often refer individuals to treatment or other resources, frequently their limited time and massive caseloads do not allow for the monitoring, advocacy, and crisis intervention required of clinical case managers (CSAT, 2004).

For treatment professionals it is often difficult to work with individuals who present with multiple and complex needs. Clinicians may retreat from these 'difficult' clients because the work can be overwhelming and frustrating when the needs of the individual are far greater than the resources available. Women involved in the criminal justice embody these multiple needs and are a minority within the treatment systems similar to the minority they represent within the criminal justice system.

Criminal Justice System Operations

Perhaps most salient to the women involved in the criminal justice system and in the community–and their treatment providers–may be the supervision they experience. Generally reporting requirements mandate those under supervision to monthly contact meetings with their supervising agent. At these meetings the agent reviews the orders of probation/parole to determine if the person is in compliance. Noncompliance with any aspect of the order–including failure to obtain or remain in treatment and use of illegal drugs (31.5% of the CJ group)–can be considered a violation. In turn, violations can be cause for incarceration.

Treatment providers are rarely trained in understanding the various dispositions along the criminal justice continuum or that treatment failure might have such weighty consequences. In addition to the multiple needs someone involved in the criminal justice system may exhibit, understanding what that involvement means to the individual and how that criminal justice sanction may (or may not) motivate them is an important clinical issue. Understanding of these nuances requires specific training of our professional workforce.

Similarly, criminal justice staff such as probation and parole agents may not be trained in assessing treatment needs–or understanding the treatment system–and underassessment has been related to parole failure

(Schram, Koons-Witt, Williams & McShane, 2006). One particular area that criminal justice personnel might contribute to effective treatment is to screen for mental health and substance abuse problems. Although this seems as if might be routine, several criminal justice institutions and entities (e.g., jails, probation offices, courts) do not routinely screen for mental health or substance abuse treatment need. Our data illustrates that only 21.7% of women in the criminal justice group were involved in mental health treatment. However, 38% stated they had symptoms of serious depression and 32.9% reported symptoms related to PTSD. Similarly over 30% met criteria for a current SUD, but only 15% were in substance abuse treatment. Appropriate assessment and treatment of mental health and substance abuse disorders may reduce recidivism.

Furthermore, criminal justice personnel need to understand the limitations of community based treatment and the professionals providing it. A supervising agent making a referral to a mental health provider may assume that substance abuse issues would be addressed, or vice versa. However, inattention to co-occurring disorders in both the substance abuse and mental health treatment systems is an issue currently on the national radar screen (SAMHSA, 2002; 2003). Likewise, an agent may assume that resources such as transportation and childcare are implicit in a referral to a job readiness program. However, absence of those resources could negatively influence the success of the intervention and increase the possibility of criminal justice sanctions.

Stigma Associated with Conviction

In addition to the domains examined for this paper, we also need to call attention to an important distinction between women–the psychological and societal stigma associated with conviction. The stigma associated with criminal justice involvement–particularly for women with children–brings about personal shame and perceptions of discrimination (Kubiak, 2005). We could not measure some of the more common stigmatizing issues that create service needs for women in the criminal justice system such as: a child's removal or separation from a parent, the pressures associated with reunification and reentry, the stress associated with confinement or criminal justice supervision, and how the stigma associated with having a conviction may limit opportunities in the community for welfare assistance, housing or employment (Richie, 2001; O'Brien, 2001). In addition, our findings document that women involved in the criminal justice system are generally younger, of minority status with less education than women in the general population or women in treatment. All of these demographic and life characteristics create multiple and intersecting oppressed identities that women involved in the criminal justice system embody.

The theory of intersectionality (Crenshaw, 1995; 1991), grounded in a critique of feminist theory's inability to account for the different within gender experiences of women of color, is a theory of the multiplicity of effects brought about when individual's social location is defined by more than one oppressed identity (e.g., gender, race, class). The intersections of these multiple oppressed identities experienced by women involved in the criminal justice system may also limit or restrict social opportunities and create a social location that is determined by the ways in which oppressive conditions come together to define a specific experience (Hurtado, 1997). Certainly, women involved in the criminal justice system seeking treatment typically have more than one oppressed identity, including, the stigma associated with criminal deviance.

If, as our study suggests, the majority of women involved in treatment represent middle aged and well educated white women, how culturally competent are clinicians to meet the needs of multiply oppressed women entering treatment? What are the mechanisms by which clinicians understand the effects of these multiple intersections on the well being of women involved in the criminal justice system and their treatment needs?

Limitations

The secondary analysis of a national probability sample encompasses both strengths and limitations. The strengths include the ability to generalize to the U.S. population a sample large enough that it includes hundreds of women involved in the criminal justice system that are not incarcerated, but in the community. It also allows for analysis of the entire CJ group, rather than only those admitted to treatment, and provides a direct comparison to the general population as well as to those who enter treatment without a criminal justice mandate. A related weakness is that we cannot compare the community based CJ group with women that are incarcerated since the NSDUH does not sample institutionalized populations. In addition, the self-report nature of the data for socially sanctioned behaviors such as arrest and drug use means the estimates are lower bound.

Other limitations include the ability to precisely measure need in any of the domains since the survey defines the individual items within the domains. In assessing the nine domains, we used conservative estimates for each of the need areas. One example is our measure of financial need defined as those with a family income of $10,000 or less. The current poverty threshold for a family of four is $20,000 (Federal Register, 2006) and using this indicator would have included more women. However due to the lack of information on family composition we used the $10,000 figure as it was closest to the poverty threshold for a single person at $9,800.

Related to our conservative measurement of need within the domains, is the fact that neither the domains associated with the LSI–nor the NSDUH–assessed history of sexual assault, particularly childhood sexual assault. A history of sexual assault may result in major psychosocial, as well as mental health issues, for women and is particularly pervasive among women involved in the criminal justices system (Browne, Miller & Maruin, 1999; Richie & Johnsen, 1996). Moreover, our assessment did not account for depressive or trauma related symptoms in any of the groups, but rather opted instead for a more extreme measure of mental illness–SMI. Assessing these issues in less restrictive ways would have increased the level of need and the complexity of care issues.

Furthermore, our examination does not directly compare women in treatment with women who are in the criminal justice system as well as in treatment. The sample sizes would be too small for such a complex sample design. However, women involved in the criminal justice system are far more likely to experience the types of health and social sequelae associated with treatment need and therefore examining the entire group seems to be more appropriate than limiting our examination to those who received treatment within the past year. A more direct and in-depth comparison should be conducted in the future.

CONCLUSION

Expanding the dialogue on gender responsive strategies to include possible within gender differences of those involved in community based treatment seems prudent as we move towards more community based sanctions (Hser, Teruya, & Evans, 2003) and re-entry initiatives (Seiter & Kadela, 2003). Certainly gender responsive strategies within institutional as well as community settings is important. However, neglecting the complex needs of women within the criminal justice system–as well as their criminal justice status–may be a disservice to women trying to maintain probation or parole sentences within the community. If our goal involves tertiary prevention–or preventing additional sequelae–we need to work with policy advocates on behalf of women in the criminal justice system to construct an effective service delivery system that keeps women sentenced to community supervision from failure and moving further along the criminal justice continuum to incarceration. This service delivery system should encompass an integrated model that includes criminal justice, mental health, substance abuse treatment systems as well as needed ancillary services such as job training, child care and physical health care. Finally workforce development initiatives need to train service professional personnel so they are equipped to understand the complex needs these women present with, as well as the multiplicative effect of the intersection of these multiple oppressed identities. This training may improve efficacious services that could in turn prevent the separation of families, loss of income, and improved supportive social networks.

This study assessed the similarities and differences between women involved in the criminal justice system and other individuals in the community seeking treatment services, and found significant differences between women involved in the criminal justices system versus those that are not. The fit between available community resources and supports and the complex and multiple needs of women involved in the criminal justice system deserves to be examined more fully in each community. Gender responsive strategies are important, but differences within gender need to be examined both at an individual treatment level and at a systems level when planning and implementing 'situationally responsive' community-based services.

REFERENCES

American Psychiatric Association (2001). *Diagnostic and Statistical Manual of Mental Disorders, 4th Edition, Revised.* Washington, D.C., American Psychiatric Association.

Andrews, D. A., Bonta, J., & Wormith, J. S. (2006). The recent past and near future of risk and/or need assessment. *Crime & Deliquency, 52,* 7-27.

Andrews, D. A. & Bonta, J. (2003). *The psychology of criminal conduct* (3rd ed.). Cincinnati: Anderson.

Andrews, D. A. & Bonta, J. (1995). *The Level of service inventory-revised.* Toronto: Multi-Health Systems.

Arfken, C. L., Klein, C., di Menza, S., & Schuster, C. R. (2001). Gender differences in problem severity at assessment and treatment retention. *Journal of Substance Abuse Treatment, 20,* 53-57.

Belenko, S. (2006). Assessing released inmates for substance-abuse related service needs. *Crime & Delinquency, 52,* 94-113.

Bloom, B., Owen, B., & Covington, S. (2003). *Gender-responsive strategies: Research, practice, and guiding principles for women offenders.* (NIC Publication No. 018017). Washington D.C.: National Institute of Corrections.

Browne, A., Miller, B., & Maguin, E. (1999). Prevalence and severity of lifetime physical and sexual victimization among incarcerated women. *International Journal of Law and Psychiatry, 22*, 301-322.

Center for Substance Abuse Treatment (CSAT) (2004). *Comprehensive case management for substance abuse treatment.* U.S. Department of Health and Human Services. Substance Abuse and Mental Health Services Administration; TIP #27. Rockville, MD.

Center for Substance Abuse Treatment (CSAT) (1999). *Substance abuse treatment for women offenders: Guide to promising practices.* U.S. Department of Health and Human Services. Substance Abuse and Mental Health Services Administration; TAP #23. Rockville, MD.

Center for Substance Abuse Treatment (CSAT) (1994). *Practical approaches in the treatment of women who abuse alcohol and other drugs.* U.S. Department of Health and Human Services. Substance Abuse and Mental Health Services Administration, Rockville, MD.

Crenshaw, K. (1991). Demarginalizing the intersection of race and sex: A black feminist critique of antidiscrimination doctrine, feminist theory, and antiracist politics. Bartlett. K, & R. Kennedy (Editors), *Feminist legal theory: Readings in law and gender.* San Francisco: Westview Press.

Crenshaw, K. W. (1995). Mapping the margins: Intersectionality, identity politics and violence against women of color. K. W. Crenshaw, N. Gotanda, G. Peller, & K. Thomas (Editors), *Critical Race Theory: The Key Writings That Formed the Movement.* New York: The New York Press.

Dowden, C. & Andrews, D. A. (1999). What works for female offenders: A Meta-analytic review. *Crime & Delinquency, 45*, 438-452.

Federal Register. (2006). Vol. 71, No. 15, January 24, 2006, 3848-3849.

Greenfield, L. A. & Snell, T. L. (1999). *Special report on women offenders.* Bureau of Justice Statistics: U.S. Department of Justice.

Griffin, M. L. & Armstrong, G. S. (2003). The effect of local life circumstances on female probationers offending. *Justice Quarterly, 20*, 213-239.

Hare-Mustin, R. T. & Marecek, J. (1998). The meaning of difference: Gender theory, postmodernism, and psychology. In B. M Clinchy & J. K. Norem (eds), *The Gender and Psychology Reader* (pp. 125-143). New York University Press, New York.

Holsinger, A. M., Lowenkamp, C. T., & Latessa, E. J. (2003). Ethnicity, gender, and the Level of Service Inventory-Revised. *Journal of Criminal Justice, 31*, 309-320.

Holtfreter, K. & Morash, M. (2003). The needs of women offenders: Implications for correctional programming. *Women & Criminal Justice, 14*, 137-160.

Hser Y. I., Teruya, C., Evans E. A., Longshore, D., Grella, C., & Garabee, D. (2003). Treating drug-abusing offenders. Initial findings from a five-county study on the impact of California's Proposition 36 on the treatment system and patient outcomes. *Evaluation Review, 27*, 479-505.

Hurtado, A. (1997). Understanding multiple group identities: Inserting women into cultural transformations. *Journal of Social Issues, 53*, 299-328.

Jordan, K., Schlenger, W., Fairbank, J., & Caddell, J. (1996). Prevalence of psychiatric disorders among incarcerated women. *Archives of General Psychiatry, 53*, 513-519.

Kessler, R. C., Andrews, G., Colpe, L. J., Hiripi, E., Mroczek, D. K., Normand, S. L. et al. (2002). Short screening scales to monitor population prevalences and trends in non-specific psychological distress. *Psychological Medicine, 32,* 959-976.

Kessler, R. C., Berglund, P., Demler, O., Jin, R., Merikangas, K. R., Walters, E. E. (2005). Lifetime prevalence and age-of-onset distributions of DSM-IV disorders in the National Comorbidity Survey Replication. *Archives General Psychiatry, 62,* 593-602.

Kubiak, S. P. (2005). Cumulative adversity and multiple traumas of women of a particular social location. *American Journal of Orthopsychiatry, 75,* 451-465.

Kubiak, S. P., Siefert, K., & Boyd, C. (2004). Empowerment and public policy: An exploration of the implications of Section 115 of the Personal Responsibility and Work Opportunity Act. *Journal of Community Psychology, 32,* 127-144.

O'Brien, P. (2001). *Making it in the "free world."* Albany: State University of Albany Press.

Richie, B. E. (2001). Challenges incarcerated women face as they return to their communities: Findings from life history interviews. *Crime and Delinquency, 47*(3), 368-389.

Richie, B. E. & Johnsen, C. (1996). Abuse histories among newly incarcerated women in a New York City jail. *Journal of the American Medical Women's Association 51*(3), 111-117.

Schram, P. J., Koons-Witt, B. A., Williams, F. P., & McShane, M. D. (2006). Supervision strategies and approaches for female parolees: Examining the link between unmet needs and parolee outcome. *Crime & Delinquency, 52,* 450-471.

Seiter R. P. & Kadela K. (2003). Prisoner Reentry: What works, what does not, and what is promising. *Crime & Delinquency 49,* 360-388.

Substance Abuse and Mental Health Services Administration. (2002). *Report to Congress on the prevention and treatment of co-occurring substance abuse disorders and mental disorders.* U.S. Department of Health and Human Services; Rockville, MD.

Substance Abuse and Mental Health Services Administration (2003). "Co-occurring disorders: Integrated Dual Disorders Treatment." *Evidence-based practices: Shaping mental health services towards recovery.* Retrieved January 4, 2005 from http://www.mentalhealth.samhsa.gov.

Substance Abuse and Mental Health Association. (2003). *Treatment Episode Data Set.* US Department of Health and Human Services. Retrieved January 2006 online at *http://wwwdasis.samhsa.gov/teds03/2003_teds_highlights.pdf.*

Teplin, L., Abram, K., & McClelland, G. (1996). Prevalence of Psychiatric Disorders Among Incarcerated Women: Pretrial Jail Detainees. *Archives of General Psychiatry, 53,* 505-512.

VanVoorhis, P., Peiler, J., Presser, L., Spiropoulis, G., & Sutherland, J. (2001). Classification of Women Offenders: A national assessment of current practices and the experiences of three states. Cincinnati, OH: University of Cincinnati, Center for Criminal Justice Research. Retrieved online September, 2005 at *http://www.nicic.org/ Misc/URLShell.aspx?SRC=Catalog&REFF=http://nicic.org/Library/017502&ID= 017502&TYPE=PDF&URL=http://www.nicic.org/pubs/2001/017502.pdf.*

Wellisch, J., Prendergast, M. L,. & Anglin, M. (1994). *Drug-Abusing Women Offenders: Results of a National Survey.* Washington, D.C.: U.S. Department of Justice.

doi:10.1300/J012v17n02_06

Maximizing Success for Drug-Affected Women After Release from Prison: Examining Access to and Use of Social Services During Reentry

Patricia O'Brien

SUMMARY. This paper describes the characteristics related to women's drug-use, criminal offending and incarceration and examines the policy and community contexts that shape their reentry after release from prison or jail. A qualitative study of formerly detained or incarcerated drug-affected women describes identified needs for services and employment as well as the challenges related to a disempowering environment. doi:10.1300/J012v17n02_07 *[Article copies available for a fee from The Haworth Document Delivery Service: 1-800-HAWORTH. E-mail address: <docdelivery@haworthpress.com> Website: <http://www.HaworthPress.com> © 2006 by The Haworth Press, Inc. All rights reserved.]*

KEYWORDS. Drug use, crime, incarceration, reentry

Patricia O'Brien, PhD, is Associate Professor, University of Illinois at Chicago, Jane Addams College of Social Work.

Address correspondence to: Patricia O'Brien, University of Illinois at Chicago, 1040 W. Harrison (M/C 309), Chicago, IL 60607 (E-mail: pob@uic.edu).

This study was funded by Grant Number R01-DA013943 from the National Institute on Drug Abuse. The opinions contained herein are those of the author and do not necessarily represent the official position of the National Institutes of Health or the National Institute on Drug Abuse.

[Haworth co-indexing entry note]: "Maximizing Success for Drug-Affected Women After Release from Prison: Examining Access to and Use of Social Services During Reentry." O'Brien, Patricia. Co-published simultaneously in *Women & Criminal Justice* (The Haworth Press, Inc.) Vol. 17, No. 2/3, 2006, pp. 95-113; and: *Drugs, Women, and Justice: Roles of the Criminal Justice System for Drug-Affected Women* (ed: James A. Swartz, Patricia O'Brien, and Arthur J. Lurigio) The Haworth Press, Inc., 2006, pp. 95-113. Single or multiple copies of this article are available for a fee from The Haworth Document Delivery Service [1-800-HAWORTH, 9:00 a.m. - 5:00 p.m. (EST). E-mail address: docdelivery@haworthpress.com].

INTRODUCTION

Nationally, women represent a growing corrections population. According to the Bureau of Justice Statistics (Glaze & Palla, 2005; Harrison & Beck, 2005), more than 1.1 million women are currently under criminal justice supervision in the United States with 91% of those on probation or parole. However, over the last thirty years women entered federal and state prisons in the U.S. in alarming numbers. During the period 1977 through the end of 2004 the population of incarcerated women has increased 757 percent, nearly twice the 388 percent increase of the male incarcerated population during this same period. In Illinois this increase was documented as 893% with an annual percentage change of 10.6% per year (Frost, Greene, & Pranis, 2006).

In addition, the disproportionate number of African American women in prison is a critical concern. The likelihood that a woman will go to prison during her lifetime has increased from a 0.3% chance in 1974 to a 1.8% chance in 2001 (Bonczar, 2003) however, the likelihood of an African American woman going to prison is much higher than that of white women: 5.6% chance as compared to less than 1% respectively.

Among criminal justice populations, women are more likely than men to use drugs, to use more serious drugs, and to use them more frequently (Kassebaum, 1999). In state prisons, about half of the women had been using drugs, alcohol, or both at the time of the offense for which they had been committed (Greenfeld & Snell, 1999). By the end of 2003, almost 65% of African American women in federal prisons were incarcerated for drug offenses (Pastore & Maguire, 2005).

The intersection of race, gender, drugs and public policy creates multiple obstacles to recovery from drug problems and desistence from further criminal behavior. This article describes some of the correlates of drug-affected women and their involvement in the criminal justice system and findings from a qualitative study of drug-convicted African American women who returned from prison to an economically disinvested community in Chicago.

POLICY CONTEXT OF INCREASING INCARCERATION

Policy analysts describe the massive increase in the numbers of incarcerated women as "collateral damage" in America's "war on drugs" beginning with President Reagan's Comprehensive Crime Control Act of 1984 aimed at street-level users and ratcheted up over the next twenty years as a normative law enforcement response to crime (Mauer & Chesney-Lind, 2003). Mandatory minimum sentences at the federal and state levels contributed to the rapid growth in the number of incarcerated women. Prior to the enactment of these "get tough" laws, judges had the discretion to consider women's roles and to modify or suspend their sentences if they felt that women should be held less responsible in a particular case.

As Britton (forthcoming) discusses, these laws served to widen the net of those charged for equal responsibility for drug sales, regardless of their actual roles in transactions. Although these laws are written as sex-neutral, in application, it has often meant that wives and girlfriends have been charged in conspiracy cases in which their only roles have been their association with the men who actually controlled drug sales.

In addition, analogous with women's positions in the "legitimate' labor force, women working within illegitimate drug operations, often have little power and therefore little information to mitigate their sentences. Bernstein (2005) reported from a study by the *Minneapolis Star Tribune* that reviewed some sixty thousand federal drug sentences and found that many women are caught on the "fringes of America's war on drugs" and "wind up serving longer prison sentences than the men who organize, lead and supply the organizations" (p. 37).

Many writers have described the structural and environmental forces that have an impact on women's criminal involvement. Arnold (1990) asserts that the detained African American women that she studied "were victims of class, gender, and race oppression who were structurally dislocated from major social institutions such as family, school and work" (p.155). Richie (1996) also discusses the "entrapment" into crime by abusers and by gender, race and class oppression. Once entrapped and criminalized, women are re-victimized and subjected to "enforcement violence" by the state through coercive laws (Bush-Baskette, 2000), social welfare policies (McCorkel, 2004) and law enforcement practice (Bhattacharjee, 2001).

Golden (2005) discusses the multiple stigmas and categories assigned to poor mothers such as "unfit" or "unworthy" that separate individual women from the mainstream culture. These cumulative stigmas converge in what she labels as "social exclusion." In her description of the correctional system as a "war on the family," she raises the "pregnant black crackhead" as the archetypal unfit mother who has been criminalized "for their failure to represent maternal integrity and family values" (p. 46). The point she makes is not that drug use during pregnancy is safe, but rather that crack babies, identified exclusively with poor, African American mothers, became a racialized gloss for punishing them and shaping public support for increased incarceration rather than treatment.

TREATMENT ISSUES AND NEEDS
FOR CRIMINALLY INVOLVED WOMEN

Arvanites (1994) found in a survey of approximately 1,600 individuals receiving treatment for drug and/or alcohol addiction that criminal activity was most frequently related to the use/abuse of alcohol in combination with at least one illicit drug. Females were more likely to report using cocaine than males (73% to 65%).

Pelissier (2004) observed gender differences in the predictors of drug treatment entry and completion during incarceration. While women had more problems in employment and depression and were more likely to have a history of physical abuse, they also had higher levels of internal motivation. Women with "average/good" family ties and those who were planning to live with their minor children after release were more likely to enter treatment. Pelissier (2004) concluded that as motivation leads to change, for women, "motivational programs and treatment programs will need to clearly emphasize the role of substance abuse treatment in alleviating depression and other psychological distress" (p. 1423).

Classification of women under criminal justice control continues to be based upon men's level of risk and does not reflect the various situational needs of women (see Kubiak & Arfken this issue; VanVoorhis, 2001). Classification matters for women exiting prison as it has an impact on the services and treatment women have access to during incarceration as well as institutional adjustment (Pogrebin & Dodge, 2001). Institutional adjustment has an impact on "good time" counted toward early release as well as recommendations for parole conditions.

Recent studies suggest there is an increasing recognition for services targeting women's specific issues such as trauma exposure related to substance abuse among jail detainees (Green, Miranda, Daroowalla, & Siddique, 2005), and examination of childhood maltreatment, adult victimization, and co-occurrence of mental health problems and drug abuse among women prisoners (Mullings, Pollock, & Crouch, 2002).

O'Brien (2002), reporting from an evaluation of a residential program for formerly incarcerated women (90% African American in a five-year sample of participants), found a high level of success for women who had longer than average stays at the program and at exit had employment, housing, and an assigned mentor. Johnson (2003) reported from a later study of women at the same program that the "structured support provided by a halfway house can enable women to develop skills for self-sufficiency as well as skills to understand and cope with past histories of physical or sexual abuse, and of substance abuse" (p. 275).

RECIDIVISM/REINTEGRATION

Returning prisoners in Illinois have many needs as they begin the process of reintegration, and the likelihood of recidivating is high. In Illinois the rates of recidivism, as defined by return to prison, is higher than the national rate for both men and women (55.3% and 48.2% respectively; Illinois Department of Corrections [IDOC], 2004). As Table 1 indicates, nationally men recidivate at a higher rate than women overall during the three years after release from prison though the trend from rearrest to reincarceration is parallel (Langan & Levin 2002).

Research has identified the specific factors contributing to women's failure or success after release from prison. Success during reentry is linked to the identification of substance abuse problems at intake (Dowden & Blanchette, 2002), social support (Farrell, 2000), communication training (Englander-Golden, Gitchel, Henderson, Golden, & Hardy 2002),

TABLE 1. Recidivism of Formerly Incarcerated Women and Men Released in 1994

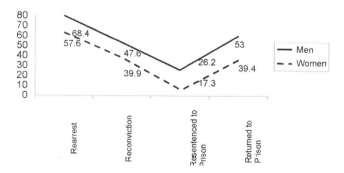

Source: Langan & Levin (2002). Recidivism of inmates released in 1994.

community-based treatment immediately after discharge (Hall, Baldwin, & Pendergast, 2001), and the use of community-based social services (Jones & Sims, 1997). In addition, findings from the Harm and Phillips study (2001), consistent with an experimental study in California (Prendergast, Wellisch, & Falkin, 1995), emphasize the need for drug-affected women to have access to both prison-based and community drug-based treatment programs.

Holtfretter and Morash (2003) and Pelissier, Camp, Gaes, Saylor, and Rhodes (2003) found that the highest risk for recidivism are more likely to have mental health needs or a history of mental health treatment. They are also most likely to have additional needs, such as those related to employment or educational services.

COMMUNITY CONTEXT

The community context of women's reentry can have an important impact on post-release success or failure. The majority of prisoners in Illinois return to the metropolitan area of Chicago after release. Just six of Chicago's 77 communities accounted for 34 percent of prisoners returning to Chicago in 2001. These neighborhoods tend to be more economically and socially disadvantaged than the average Chicago community being populated by more families below the poverty line, a higher percentage of female-headed households, a higher rate of un-employment, a higher rate of crime, and a higher rate of renter-occupied housing (La Vigne & Mamalian, 2003).

Community-based programming is offered by the state through elec-tronic detention as a prerelease reintegration technique, through adult transition centers (none of the centers for women are located in Chicago) and a day reporting center on the south side of Chicago where releases can participate in educational, employment, treatment, and life skills programming. As is true of most states, Illinois received a U.S. Depart-ment of Justice grant to support a prisoner reentry program. The Illinois program is focused on working with young male violent offenders released to Chicago. Another federally and state-funded program has totally revamped one of the prisons in Illinois to provide a specialized drug treatment and job training milieu for all male inmates at the facility.

There is also a relatively rich network of not-for-profit agencies throughout the greater Chicago metropolitan area that provide assis-tance to parolees. However, as La Vigne and Mamalian (2003) concluded from their "portrait of prisoner reentry in Illinois" the wide array of programs designed to increase the likelihood that inmates returning to their communities will reintegrate successfully are not sufficient to meet former inmates' needs. In addition to the insufficient availability and comprehensiveness of community-based services, the lack of an economic infrastructure that enables people to regain a foothold for reentry, particularly in neighborhoods where drug use and sales are an obvious part of everyday life, is a serious challenge. This article builds upon previous research on women's identified needs after release from prison and an exploratory study of women's return to one community in Chicago in order to understand better the issues related to how women can improve their prospects for successful reentry.

STUDY OF REENTRY IN AN URBAN NEIGHBORHOOD

The intent of the exploratory study was to investigate the experiences of drug-convicted women returning to a particular community in Chicago and to examine both how the individual women described their needs and what informal and formal community supports assisted these women to stay out of prison. In addition, the study investigated how community-based providers described available social support, housing and economic opportunities for women returning from prison or jail. The study aimed to address three questions:

- What happens when drug-affected, newly released women return to an under-resourced urban community?
- How do women reach beyond what they see in their daily environments for support in their recovery from addiction and desistence from further criminal involvement?
- What do community-based service providers describe as necessary for women to be successful in reentry?

The study also used a critical standpoint to examine how the observed intersection of race, gender and poverty has an impact on women who are attempting to reconstruct their lives after serving their sentences.

Sample and Data Collection Methods

The neighborhood of Cameron[1] was chosen as a focus for the study as it was identified as one of six communities in the metropolitan Chicago area where as discussed previously, a high number of former inmates return after release from prison. Census figures from 2000 describe Cameron as a low income neighborhood that on every major indicator (female-headed households, unemployment, crime rate and poverty rate) ranks "worse than" the average for the city of Chicago (U.S. Census Bureau, 2000).

Although Golden (2005) refers to this neighborhood (which between 1991 and 2000 lost nearly 3,000 jobs) as "abandoned by hope" (p. 24), it is also a community of visionaries and warriors who won't give up on the dream of a revitalized and safe neighborhood. Thus, it provides both the crippling reality of a dissolving economic base and drug-infested alleys coincident with churches and community centers where the faith for a better day is daily ignited. These contrasting community characteristics can serve as either risks or as protective factors for women attempting to reclaim their lives after exit from prison.

A convenience sample of thirteen women was recruited for the study. They had all been convicted of drug possession or trafficking, had been released from prison or jail within the past three months of the study period and were living in the identified neighborhood. Study participants heard about the study by referral from social service agencies, from posted flyers, or from other participants. The thirteen study respondents were all African American, with an average age of 38.7 (ranging from 21 to 52 years old) and an average of three biological children under the age of 18.

We interviewed the thirteen women at two different points in time approximately three (average 95 days) and six months (average 184 days out) after release. A schedule of questions was used to guide each interview. The face-to-face interviews were held in respondents' homes or the study office and lasted from an hour to an hour and a half. The interviews were audio taped and transcribed. The four study team members were trained in using qualitative interviewing strategies. In order to retain the sample from the first interview to the second interview we used strategies such as assigning the same interviewer for each time and encouraging contact between interviews to build rapport. The study was approved by the University Institutional Review Board and because we were asking sensitive questions about illicit behavior that could result in revocation of parole or new charges, we also got a Certificate of Confidentiality to provide the women additional protection from violation of confidentiality.

The first interview was focused on the life history of the respondent, critical events (defined as events that she recalled as causing her great stress or difficulty) in her life, her current alcohol and drug use, and her current appraisal of her situation. The first interview also included an embedded brief scale for detecting psychiatric disorders (Kessler et al.,

2002). The second interview questions focused on any changes the women described since the first interview including alcohol or drug use, residence, employment, and social service or treatment use and proximity of location and access to services.

We also conducted semi-structured phone interviews with five nominated service providers who provide employment, health, emergency shelter, and support services to former prisoners and/or to drug-affected women in the neighborhood in which the women resided. These questions focused on the provider's assessment of current services including challenges and recommendations for other needed services.

Data Analysis

The analysis of the interview narratives with the women in the sample included both a descriptive matrix of simple frequencies related to critical life events, alcohol and drug initiation and use, an individual "lifeline" for each woman, and a thematic analysis using an open coding framework derived from the search for recurrent patterns related to individual, interactional and social structural elements in each woman's responses. In addition, we mapped data points where women identified social service and health resources that they used to document proximity of services. Analysis of the five service providers' responses followed a similar thematic review based on the template of questions asked and answered in the brief phone exchanges; these agency locations were also mapped in order to document their proximity to the study respondents' locations as well as to the other identified service locations.

Findings

Descriptive profile. Table 2 summarizes some of the characteristics of the sample of women respondents. Women reported an average of 5.23 of what they identified as critical life events (range was from 2 to 13). These events included child molestation, unplanned pregnancy, abusive relationships as adults, extreme physical injury during childhood, loss of a child due to violent means, loss of a child by abortion or miscarriage, unexpected death of a parent or significant family member, death of an intimate partner or spouse, multiple suicide attempts, and multiple incarcerations. We attempted to understand how the critical life events related to initiation of and continuation of substance use, the need for drug treatment and other forms of services, and the use of treatment and services.

TABLE 2. Selected Summary Characteristics

Item	Mean
Age at first use of alcohol	14
Age of first pregnancy	16
Age at first use of illegal drug	18
Years of completed education	11.2
K-6 score	7.9
Number of critical life events	5.23

Women in the sample initiated alcohol use at age 14; four respondents connected initial alcohol use (usually with an older male) to becoming pregnant for the first time and then dropping out of school. Nine of the women reported unexpected pregnancies; the average age for first pregnancy was 16 and the range was 13 to 20 for the group, lower than the national mean for African-American women of 22.6 (Martin, Hamilton, Sutton, et al., 2003). Respondents initiated drug use at the average age of 18 not an atypical age for first use though the range was from age 12 to 26. One woman in the sample was convicted for drug possession plead down from a drug sales charge; she reported not ever using alcohol or drugs. Most of the women who used drugs (11 of the 13) reported misusing alcohol and using either crack cocaine or heroin (though several indicated that their start-up drug was marijuana).

When assessed on the K-6 brief scale at the first interview, two women reported symptoms of psychological distress consistent with a serious mental illness with another four women reporting a moderate degree of psychological distress. Though the average score on the K-6 was 7.9, the range was 0 (no distress) to 24 (highest distress).

At the first interview, three months after release from prison, 69% of the sample reported they were misusing alcohol (1 woman) or using illicit drugs (8 women). At the second interview about three months later, only thirty-one percent (4) reported they were still using. Two of the women who were still using were also the most highly distressed according to the K-6 scale.

Women's survival and post-prison resilience. Women's narratives of their life history prior to involvement with the criminal justice system were marked by family dislocation and loss, extreme violence, illness, injury and addiction. Table 3 indicates the number of each of these events among this group of women.

TABLE 3. Critical Life Events (n = 13)

Early pregnancy	Quit high school	Loss of parent before age 20	Use of alcohol befcre 15	Use of drugs before 21	Death of significant family member	Death of husband/ partner	Sexual molestation/ assault (child)	Intimate partner violence (adult)	Psychiatric hospitalization/ Suicide attempts	More than 1 prison sentence
9	4	4	6	9	7	3	3	8	5	10

We created life lines for each of the respondents as a way to further examine the trajectory of critical life events and the inception or continued use of alcohol and/or drugs. Space limitations prevent reporting all of those life lines in this article but the following represent two members of the sample: the youngest (21) and the oldest (52) and provides additional descriptive information.

#1 "victim of circumstances," Class 1 possession of a controlled substance.

1983	1998	1999	2002	2004
Born	"ended up pregnant"	stop school	2nd child 1st arrest	Interviews

This respondent defined critical events as "my surroundings before I got incarcerated." She indicated that she was not a drug user but a "people pleaser" that prevented her from evicting drug dealers from her residence. She displayed no apparent mental health problems and referred often to her spiritual beliefs. Even though she had not completed high school, she had received her General Education Diploma. By the second interview, she had used a referral to a social service agency that assisted her with obtaining employment. At that interview she reported, "I don't take the same things off people. People say to me, you're not the same. I'm not going to get into any trouble for nobody."

#12 "heroin can be like your boyfriend"

1952	1968	1972	1976	1992	2003	2004
Born	first use Marijuana	birth to son	1st arrest assault Selling/using heroin	boyfriend murdered	incarcerated 10th time	Interview 1-still using Interview 2-not using

In the first interview, this respondent reported feeling isolated and cut-off from others and that heroin enabled her to "do more." By the second interview, she reported following some leads for employment interviews (though she was not yet working), that she had received clothing from a neighbor and concrete assistance from her father to pay her rent and support from her son to "go straight." When asked why she had apparently stopped using without any further treatment, she indicated that she didn't have an addiction, and that:

> I don't want to go back, I lost too much when I went, my respect, my apartment, my furniture. I lost a lot. I can't do the same thing. I don't look for that dope to make me happy or fill my life's voids. I try to figure out what they are and do something else.

However, two other women reported that being in the neighborhood specifically triggered their continued using: "Drugs, shooting and other things that are going on–it's really not a good neighborhood like it was when I first moved there." Another said in referring to the typical heroin user, "People just nodding and it looked good." About half of the women reported not wanting to go out in the neighborhood for fear of getting caught up in the drug activities outside of their door.

Four of the women at the first interview talked about the difficulty of "having nothing to do" along with most of the women who expressed their belief that "nobody would hire me" due to their drug use and criminal record. One woman honestly reported "My mind wasn't made up to just leave it alone–that's the whole thing." Some of the women seemed to acquiesce to a label they perceived had already been applied to them. Employment symbolized not only legitimate income, but also "something to do" that enabled them to manage boredom or loneliness.

> As one woman said, "Life is staring at me. It's bleak. When they find out you've been locked up, I never get people to answer me back."

At the time of the first interview, all of the women were living in someone else's home. They mostly lived with family members who were also still caring for the women's children. It was this need for housing and the fact that the women had lived in this neighborhood before prison and that it was where their friends and family members still lived that contributed to them returning to this neighborhood. If family or friends cannot provide housing, there are few alternatives for women, especially transitional shelters where they can stay with their children. A limitation of the study was that we did not further investigate the relationship the women actually had with the family members or friends with whom they lived. In most of the interviews, there seemed to be some unarticulated tension or a sense of staying apart from other members in the household.

By the time of the second interview, six months after release, only four women were still using illegal substances. Four of the women were employed at least part-time. Two of the women were enrolled in employment training or a job readiness program. As one of the newly employed women said indicating some of the personal efficacy that she felt in relationship to getting a part-time homemaker job:

> I'm healthy. I'm young. I'm able to do a lot of things. I have a lot of skills. I like just knowing that I can get the job done and be satisfied and the person I'm doing the job for is satisfied with me.

Another woman reported the string of successes that she believed came from getting the job:

> I just got a job and right after I got a job, I got a car. Everything just fell into place. I'm stable, I'm not making a whole lot of money but I'm doing just fine.

The one woman who reported that she was in a combination GED/job training program talked about the relief she felt in delaying her job search so that she could stay focused on completing her GED:

> That was my main problem, by my wanting a job so bad. Now I know I have to be patient and to wait on the job I want. If the job that I want don't come along and another job comes, ok, I'll go for that job until the I get the job I really want because I know now that I need more computer training and I really need my GED.

Most of the women did not enroll in drug treatment. Seeking drug treatment may have been a court or parole condition, but because there was a scarcity of drug treatment options (and none in the immediate neighborhood where the women resided) and because there was a reported lack of follow-up by parole officers or court personnel, only three of the women were in some type of drug treatment program. The services that five women reported using provided immediate and concrete goods such as food and clothing. Several women engaged in peer groups that may have also supported their efforts to stay clean.

What else accounted for desistance for those who reported they were no longer using? For some, it may have been the fact that they had something else "to do" such as employment or training. Two of the women had moved outside of the neighborhood and believed they had some new opportunities. Some others reported they were "sick and tired of the same situation" and wanting something better for themselves. Several women mentioned the importance of their children having a model for not using drugs especially when they recognized with some pride that their children had not gotten "caught up" so far in drugs or other problems. Women also described increased relational competence in making choices about when and how they spent time with others, and a sense of efficacy in being able to resist further illicit activities.

Community Based-Service Providers

Phone interviews were conducted with five service providers who served the neighborhood where the women resided. These respondents worked at agencies that provided employment services, short term transitional residential shelter, health services, and education (Adult Basic Education and GED). Service providers reported they could assist formerly incarcerated women with health care, public transportation, temporary housing, childcare, job placement assistance, case management, referrals for psychological or drug treatment, safety and support. They also identified gaps in services related to family counseling and restoration, ongoing peer support, stable housing, and a "different environment" that would be conducive to prosocial living. As one respondent said, "whatever was there has not changed. It's like you're putting new seed in old soil–no nutrients to support new growth."

Several providers discussed the social and structural needs that went beyond services that could foster and reinforce beginning steps toward wholeness especially to support women in resuming their mothering role. There was a recognition that women had not been given the attention that had been focused on the men coming back to the same neighborhood, and that had made it difficult for women to reach out for assistance.

CONCLUSION

This paper provides a synthesis of literature that describes the complex issues that African American women involved with the criminal justice system experience as well as findings from a study with women and service providers in one neighborhood in a large, urban city heavily marked by the issues of continuing illicit drug use, low education and employment rates and a high proportion of formerly incarcerated community members.

Although census figures from 2000 describe this primarily African-American neighborhood as beset by multiple negative indicators, it is also a neighborhood that is ripe for economic and social change. In addition to an emerging faith-based network, a thriving community newspaper, and several new housing complexes that include subsidized and market-rate homes and rental units, it has fostered the growth of a major partnership of community-based organizations, economic development agencies and businesses working together to "improve the earnings potential of the community through innovative employment initiatives that lead to economic advancement and an improved quality of life for residents." The neighborhood also hosts one of the few programs in the city explicitly designed for former prisoners, an employment and case management program that since its inception has attracted far more men than women but is now attempting to expand its outreach to women.

Based on the interviews with women and service providers the following recommendations should be considered when attempting to be facilitative of formerly incarcerated women's reentry after incarceration in jail or prison.

1. a comprehensive and multidimensional assessment of psychological, social/relational, and educational/vocational needs prior to release;
2. assistance with identifying family issues for family conferencing and negotiation;
3. closer attention to job placement that enables women to gain income and gradual experience in the labor market but also provides a manageable schedule for addressing other post-release expectations or needs.

Finally, we do not yet know the full impact of the collateral consequences of laws for ex-offenders (Finzen, 2005). Collateral consequences law makes rehabilitation challenging for former prisoners; collectively, these laws make reintegration even more difficult, if not impossible, when they intersect to exert an impact on African-American women's economic and social choices. These laws, such as restrictions on employment, public housing, and access to public benefits, adhere as a result of a criminal conviction and continue to civilly punish ex-offenders long after their sentences have ended. Without access to housing, employment, or education, it becomes nearly impossible for a formerly incarcerated woman, regardless of race to successfully reintegrate into society and turn away from criminal activities. These consequences are derived from a putative drug war that while exacting a high societal cost, no one wins.

NOTE

1. A pseudonym is used for the identified community in order to protect the confidentiality of the respondents.

REFERENCES

Arnold, R. A. (1990). Processes of victimization and criminalization of black women. *Social Justice, 17*, 153-166.

Arvanites, T. M. (1994). Female Drug Use and Crime. Presented at the American Society of Crimininology, Miami, FL, November 11, 1994.

Bernstein, N. (2005). *All alone in the world: Children of the incarcerated.* New York: New Press.

Bhattacharjee, A. (2001, May). *Whose safety? Women of color and the violence of law enforcement.* Unpublised Working Paper. Philadelphia: American Friends Service Committee on Women, Population and the Environment.

Bonczar, T. P. (2003). *Prevalence of imprisonment in the U.S. population, 1974-2001.* Washington, DC: Bureau of Justice Statistics (NCJ197976).

Britton, D. (forthcoming). *The gender of crime.* Walnut Creek, CA: Alta Mira Press.

Bush-Baskette, S. R. (2000). The war on drugs and the incarceration of mothers. *Journal of Drug Issues, 30*, 919-928.

Dodge, M., & Pogrebin, M. R. (2001). Collateral costs of imprisonment for women: Complications of reintegration. *The Prison Journal, 81*, 42-54.

Dowden, C., & Blanchette, K. (2002). An evaluation of the effectiveness of substance abuse programming for female offenders. *International Journal of Offender Therapy and Comparative Criminology, 46*, 220-230.

Englander-Golden, P., Gitchel, E., Henderson, C. E., Golden, D. E., & Hardy, R. (2002). "Say It Straight" training with mothers in chemical dependency treatment. *Journal of Offender Rehabilitation, 35*, 1-22.

Farrell, A. (2000). Women, crime, and drugs: Testing the effects of therapeutic communities. *Women & Criminal Justice, 11*, 21-48.

Finzen, M. E. (2005). Systems of oppression: the collateral consequences of incarceration and their effects on black communities. *Georgetown Journal on Poverty Law & Policy, 12*, 299-324.

Frost, N. A., Greene, J., & Pranis, K. (2006). *Hard hit: The growth in the imprisonment of women, 1977-2004.* New York: Institute on Women & Criminal Justice.

Glaze, L. E., & Palla, S. (2005). *Probation and parole in the United States, 2004.* Washington, DC: Bureau of Justice Statistics (NCJ 210676).

Golden, R. (2005). *War on the family: Mothers in prison and the families they leave behind.* New York: Routledge.

Green, B. L., Miranda, J., Daroowalla, A., & Siddique, J. (2005). Trauma exposure, mental health functioning, and program needs of women in jail. *Crime & Delinquency, 51,* 133-151.

Greenfeld, L. A., & Snell, T. L. (1999). *Women offenders.* Washington, DC: Bureau of Justice Statistics (NCJ 175688).

Hall, E. A., Baldwin, D. M., & Prendergast, M. L. (2001). Women on parole: Barriers to success after substance abuse treatment. *Human Organization, 60,* 225-233.

Harm, N. J., & Phillips, S. D. (2001). You can't go home again: Women and recidivism. *Journal of Offender Rehabilitation, 32,* 3-21.

Harrison, P. M., & Beck, A. J. (2005). *Prisoners in 2004.* Washington, DC: Bureau of Justice Statistics (NCJ210677).

Holtfreter, K., & Morash, M. (2003). The needs of women offenders: Implications for correctional programming. *Women & Criminal Justice, 14,* 137-160.

Illinois Department of Corrections. *2004 Statistical Presentation.* Retrieved July 3, 2006 from http://www.idoc.state.il.us/

Johnson, P. C. (2003). *Inner lives: Voices of African American women in prison.* New York: University Press.

Jones, M., & Sims, B. (1997). Recidivism of offenders released from prison in North Carolina: A gender comparison. *The Prison Journal, 77,* 335-348.

Kassebaum, P. A. (1999). *Substance abuse treatment for women offenders: guide to promising practice.* Rockville, MD: U.S. Department of Health and Human Services, Center for Substance Abuse Treatment.

Kessler, R. C., Andrews, G., Colpe, L. J., Hiripi, E., Miroczek, D. K., Normand, S. L., Walters, E. E., & Zaslavsky, A. (2002). Short screening scales to monitor population prevalences and trends in nonspecific psychological distress. *Psychological Medicine, 32*(6), 959-976.

Langan, P. A., & Levin D. J. (2002). *Recidivism of inmates released in 1994.* Washington, DC: Bureau of Justice Statistics. NCJ 193427.

La Vigne, N. G., & Mamalian, C. A. (2003). *A portrait of prisoner reentry in Illinois.* Washington, DC: Urban Institute.

Martin, J. A., Hamilton, B. E., Sutton, P. D., Ventura, S. J., Menacker, F., & Munson, M. L. (2003). Births: Final data for 2002. *National Vital Statistics Reports, 52.* Hyattsville, MD: National Center for Health Statistics. Retrieved July 13, 2005 from http://www.cdc.gov/nchs/data/nvsr/nvsr52/nvsr52_10.pdf.

Mauer, M., & Chesney-Lind, M. (eds.). (2003). Invisible punishment: The collateral consequences of mass incarceration. New York: Free Press.

McCorkel, J. (2004). Criminally dependent? Gender, punishment, and the rhetoric of welfare reform. *Social Politics, 11,* 386-410.

Mullings, J. L.. Pollock, J. & Crouch, B. M. (2002). Drugs and criminality: Results from the Texas women inmates study. *Women & Criminal Justice, 13,* 69-96.

O'Brien, P. (2002). *Evaluation of Grace House: Using past experience to inform future results.* Chicago, IL: Jane Addams College of Social Work.

Pastore, A. L., & Maguire, K. (2005). *Sourcebook of Criminal Justice Statistics.* Washington, DC: U.S. Department of Justice, Bureau of Justice Statistics. NCJ 208756.

Pelissier, B. (2004). Gender differences in substance use treatment entry and retention among prisoners with substance use histories. *American Journal of Public Health, 94*, 1418-1425.

Pelissier, B. M. M., Camp, S. D., Gaes, G. G., Saylor, W. G., & Rhodes, W. (2003). Gender differences in outcomes from prison-based residential treatment. *Journal of Substance Abuse Treatment, 24*, 149-160.

Pogrebin, M. R., & Dodge, M. (2001). Women's accounts of their prison experiences: A retrospective view of their subjective realities. *Journal of Criminal Justice, 29*, 531-541.

Prendergast, M. L., Wellisch, J., & Falkin, G. P. (1995). Assessment of and services for substance-abusing women offenders in community and correctional settings. *The Prison Journal, 75*, 240-256.

Richie, B. E. (1996). *Compelled to Crime: the gender entrapment of battered black women.* New York: Routledge.

U.S. Census Bureau (2000). Census 2000 Summary File. Retrieved on November 11, 2005 from http://factfinder.census.gov.

Van Voorhis, P. (2001). *Classification of Women Offenders: A national assessment of current practices.* Washington, D.C.: U.S. Department of Justice.

doi:10.1300/J012v17n02_07

Power Inside:
A Grassroots Program for Women Survivors of Traumatic Violence, the Street Economy, and the Criminal Justice System

Jacqueline Robarge

SUMMARY. This paper describes the genesis and growth of Power Inside, a community-based program in Baltimore that serves women survivors of traumatic violence, the street economy, and the criminal justice system. It examines the social context and theoretical framework that define the program. The development of the organization was based on guiding principles grounded in our desire for social change as well as a dynamic exchange of information between the program and participants to design interventions. This paper also discusses Power Inside's client-centered, community-based, and institution-based interventions that are intended to foster individual empowerment and access to justice as

Jacqueline Robarge is Program Director, Power Inside, a program of Fusion Partnerships, Inc., P.O. Box 4796, Baltimore, MD 21211 (E-mail: jacquelinerobarge@msn.com).

The author would like to thank the Maryland Department of Public Safety and Correctional Services for their collaboration; Rachel McLean, Susan Sherman and the Johns Hopkins University for their technical assistance and for conducting the WINDOW Study; and the staff, volunteers, supporters, and most importantly, the participants of Power Inside for sharing their strength, wisdom and commitment to our work.

[Haworth co-indexing entry note]: "Power Inside: A Grassroots Program for Women Survivors of Traumatic Violence, the Street Economy, and the Criminal Justice System." Robarge, Jacqueline. Co-published simultaneously in *Women & Criminal Justice* (The Haworth Press, Inc.) Vol. 17, No. 2/3, 2006, pp. 115-125; and: *Drugs, Women, and Justice: Roles of the Criminal Justice System for Drug-Affected Women* (ed: James A. Swartz, Patricia O'Brien, and Arthur J. Lurigio) The Haworth Press, Inc., 2006, pp. 115-125. Single or multiple copies of this article are available for a fee from The Haworth Document Delivery Service [1-800-HAWORTH, 9:00 a.m. - 5:00 p.m. (EST). E-mail address: docdelivery@haworthpress.com].

115

well as contribute to social change movements. Lastly, the paper suggests future directions for Power Inside. doi:10.1300/J012v17n02_08 *[Ar-
ticle copies available for a fee from The Haworth Document Delivery Service:
1-800-HAWORTH. E-mail address: <docdelivery@haworthpress.com> Website:
<http://www.HaworthPress.com> © 2006 by The Haworth Press, Inc. All rights
reserved.]*

KEYWORDS. Jail, detainees, reentry, commercial sex work, drug addiction, trauma, harm reduction, homelessness

INTRODUCTION

*Can you help me? Can you help me understand? I'm 46 years of
age and have been in the system since the mid 80's. Why? I'm a
user of drugs, yes, but I haven't always been. Now, I'm what society calls a criminal. No one is noticing who I am. I've never killed
anyone but myself. Behind the six digits that you know me as, is a
mother of one and grandmother of four begging for a fair chance
and opportunity. Why hasn't anyone looked beyond my record and
seen my tears? (B.W., personal communication used with permis-
sion, August 28, 2002)*

In early 2001, we were invited by the Baltimore City Detention Center to conduct a "self esteem" class for women in the city jail. At that
time, an investigation by the United States Department of Justice [DOJ]
Civil Rights Division (Department of Justice [DOJ], 2002) was well un-
derway. The DOJ findings released in August 2002 indicated that "persons confined suffer harm or the risk of serious harm from deficiencies
in the facility's fire safety protections, medical care, mental health care,
sanitation, opportunity to exercise and protection of juveniles" (p. 1).
Women would enter the room for the class, sick, in pain, and without
hope. The initial inquires we asked were: what should we even talk
about–what is a responsible curriculum in that setting? Should we focus
on health? Reentry? Family?

Despite not yet having a clear answer, we just began. We let popular
education (Freire, 1972) and our background in facilitating women's
empowerment groups guide us to create a space where women in the jail
were heard and taken seriously. We posed fundamental questions–*what
do women in jail need? What can be done in the community to help
women stay out of jail? What forces have influenced our collective*

circumstances? How do we create change? One by one the women shared stories of years of abuse, addiction, exploitation, poverty and lack of opportunity leading up to their incarceration.

With little access to services, and a legitimate fear of what they would face when they returned to the community, the women pushed the boundaries of the group well beyond a cursory examination of women's self esteem. The group became a place for women to support one another through the loss of a child, discuss a new diagnosis of HIV, arrange suicide watches, share street survival skills, and collect information about drug treatment and health programs. They acknowledged each other's struggles as individuals, and identified the social structures that marginalized them as a group. The collective answers to our questions became a call to action that has motivated Power Inside since its inception five years ago.

FOUNDING PRINCIPLES

Through our initial conversations with women in jail, we developed founding principles to guide our program priorities. In the most basic sense, we believe that women have human rights that include safety, dignity and justice. We witnessed the denial of human rights both inside correctional facilities and in communities created by oppression based on race, class, gender, ability, and sexual orientation. This oppression is reinforced by violence. The majority of the women we meet are survivors of domestic violence, sexual assault and/or child abuse. In addition to abuse, police brutality and sexual exploitation, forced sterilization, medical neglect, mass incarceration, and denial of access to food and shelter, are included in our definition of violence and violation of women's human rights.

The way gender-based violence and structural oppression impacted women individually seemed to implicate how many came to be institutionalized and criminalized. We see women who are largely criminalized for health and social issues such as drug addiction, mental illness, homelessness, or self-defense from domestic violence. While society incarcerates women for health issues, there is little access to services that would help them actually overcome these problems. Therefore, we were compelled not only to provide tangible resources to women and expand their ability to access those resources–but also to accomplish this with an awareness of the way in which economic and social marginalization plays out in their lives personally and collectively. Consequently, we frame our services as a health and human rights response to women's oppression and see the criminal justice system as merely the physical and theoretical locality of our work.

DEVELOPMENT OF PROGRAM

Power Inside's peer based support group began as an all-volunteer project in May 2001 inside the Baltimore City Detention Center. In November 2002, I received a fellowship to continue our program in the jail and to engage in local advocacy that would amplify the voices of women and their families who were directly impacted by the criminal justice system. For two years, I acted as facilitator, director, community organizer and client advocate meeting with up to 30 women per week in jail and in the community to lay the foundation for the project. Fusion Partnership, Inc. a small nonprofit became our host organization, and in late 2003 we received our first grants for the program making it possible to expand services. Our current funding sustains four staff members, volunteers, and administrative support.

We developed interventions to bridge gaps that exist between correctional settings and public health systems as the women we encountered identified them. For women who are incarcerated, we hope to facilitate access to a range of community-based resources prior to their release from jail or prison. Through offering health information and advocacy, we seek to empower women to reduce or eliminate the harmful consequences of drug use and street life, and provide services that offer a path to an improved quality of life. The range of services to meet those needs include workshops and support groups both inside and outside correctional facilities, case management and advocacy, a public reentry office with practical and emotional support, a young women's program, and street outreach to homeless women cycling through jail.

WINDOW STUDY

As we continued to advocate for women detained at the Baltimore City jail, we were asked to supply empirical documentation that confirmed the anecdotes upon which we based our services. Beyond an informal survey that we conducted in 2001 that found high rates of drug addiction, sex trade work, and nearly universal experiences of domestic and sexual violence among the women we served, little data existed that supported our claims. We felt that numerous accounts of limited access to education, drug treatment, health care and housing should be sufficient, but understood the demands for research where none existed could be a barrier for our program. As with any new endeavor we asked our program participants for feedback on how to move forward.

In 2003, based on our participants' directive to tell their story 'by any means necessary,' we began to develop a needs assessment. As a result, a collaboration between Power Inside, the Maryland Department of Public Safety and Correctional Services, and Johns Hopkins University Bloomberg School of Public Health (JHSPH) was formed to study the needs of women in jail who would soon be released into the community. The JHSPH study, entitled "WINDOW Study–Release from Jail: Moment of Crisis or Window of Opportunity for Female Detainees in Baltimore City?" (McLean, Robarge & Sherman, 2005)–offers the baseline findings helpful to design and evaluate projects that serve women transitioning from jail to the community, including Power Inside.

WINDOW study staff interviewed 148 women detained at the Baltimore City Detention Center. We asked women what barriers they anticipated facing upon release from jail and what services they felt would be useful to them. Upon release, almost half of the women had no stable housing where they could stay for more than 30 days. Women reported high amounts of mental illness (63.5%), recent daily heroin and cocaine use (59%), and recent commercial sex work (34%). African American women as well as women who identified as lesbian or bisexual were over-represented in comparison to Baltimore's general population. Most women did not have insurance or a legal income prior to arrest and reported high rates of chronic diseases. Of the 80% who were mothers, 58% had custody of at least one minor child. Women with family support were six times more likely to have housing when they were released from jail. The study also found that women who wanted a support group for issues surrounding sex work or who identified as lesbian or bisexual were less likely to have a place to stay.

When asked what services they needed when released from jail, health services were high on the list, including dental care (90%), health care (88%), drug treatment (74%), and counseling for past abuse (31%) and sex work (27%). Many needed preventative health care such as a gynecological exam, mammogram, or HIV test. Women believed having access to housing (88%) and employment (95%) would help keep them out of jail in the future. The WINDOW Study articulated the complex barriers women faced and has helped to hone our interventions and advocacy.

PROGRAM MODEL

Power Inside's program participants present their hopes for the future and life events, not as a set of clinical symptoms or a single barrier to overcome, but as whole people. In the simplest terms, our approach is to listen to each woman's story and her assessment of her needs, strengths and goals. We respond with validation and practical support. We have incorporated harm reduction (Marlatt, 1996), motivational interviewing (Miller & Rollnick, 2002), the transtheoretical model of change (Prochaska & DiClemente, 1984), peer support (Wilkerson, 2002), intersectionality (Crenshaw, 1991), and relational theory (Miller, 1976; Bloom, Owens & Covington, 2003) into our programming. These theoretical models guide our policies and practices in the delivery of services.

Power Inside intends to provide services that are gender and culturally specific in order to respect each woman's identity, background, health status and culture. We do not force women to disentangle life events or multiple cultural identities from their current incarceration in order to quickly name a single 'problem.' For example, when asked about her substance abuse history and what led to her incarceration, one woman shared:

> I was abused as a child and my parents got divorced but I chose to drop out of school, do drugs and run away. When I looked inside the darker area of my childhood; my drug use prevented me from dealing with it. I felt as though the world had turned its back on me. But I don't have to be the person that drugs made me be. I want this cycle to end. I don't want this to be my daughter or one of my sons. (A.K., personal communication used with permission, February 2004)

Although we are unable to immediately address such complex issues, placing an emphasis on sincerity and respect establishes a connection that is a crucial foundation for any subsequent support work. In addition, understanding each woman's perception of her history, strengths, skills, and family ties is paramount to offering appropriate services. We work to empower women who have been systemically marginalized, and who therefore have limited social support and access to resources. Women with disabilities, lesbian and bisexual women, women of color and/or young women who are also survivors of violence and drug addicted are particularly impacted. Open bias or institutionalized policies create a 'screening out' process that routinely excludes women from community, faith and governmental service agencies that historically have had difficulty acknowledging intersecting issues.

Harm reduction (Marlatt, 1996), and the transtheoretical model of change (Prochaska & DiClemente, 1984) offers Power Inside a set of evidence based practices with which to intervene with women whose lives are often physically and emotionally unsafe, such as women who use drugs, women in abusive relationships, and women who trade sex to survive. The transtheoretical model frames behavior change as a progression through stages related to an individual's readiness and motivation. This framework allows us to affirm women as they take tenuous steps toward change. We assist each participant to pursue individualized goals that are significant yet achievable—a process that often evaluates multiple risks and barriers that jeopardize their safety and health. In addition to attending to their immediate concerns, we have found harm reduction effective in engaging women in order to link them to more comprehensive or abstinence based services.

Peer support (Wilkerson, 2002) offers hope for women who are survivors of rape, domestic violence, and child abuse—staff and volunteers who have had similar experiences work with the women. As peers, Power Inside's staff members are culturally competent, non-judgmental, credible among participants, and have genuine concern. In our peer support groups, women demonstrate their desire to learn from each other and show empathy. Working with their peers, they break down barriers to healing, such as shame and isolation. We encourage women to listen to one another, request feedback, and share strategies to heal and grow. Participants often take on leadership roles within the program by making presentations, leading activities, assisting other women with low literacy, and providing input on programming. Women who are struggling to build healthy lives and reconnect with families and communities are able to practice skills and share successes within the context of a supportive community of peers.

SERVICES

Since our initial support group at the jail, we have expanded the scope of our services into the community as well as into other correctional facilities. Our goal is to have the ability to offer a continuum of support that is accessible to women as they cycle through jail back to the street or to prison, and as their environmental or social situation changes.

In the jail–Generally we meet women for the first time while they are in the Baltimore City jail. They may voluntarily join our weekly support group held in the single classroom in the facility for more than 600 women. We receive referrals from facility staff, community based organizations, and family members, and by letter from women within the institution. In our first encounter, we establish rapport and briefly screen each woman to assess her post-release needs and understand her access–or lack thereof–to resources. We have adapted our jail-based program to the brevity of encounters, health of participants, institutional policies, and physical space in order to connect with women in jail. Rarely do we have the opportunity to meet with women at length in a private counseling space. Because it is likely a woman in jail will soon be released, we immediately gather essential contact information and begin transition planning. Frequently, time will only allow for planning for the first hours and days after release. We make referrals to prevent homelessness, health crises and drug relapse, arrange transportation and linkages, and schedule appointments in the community.

In each successive meeting, whether it is one or eight sessions, we continue to build trust, gather information and offer increasingly comprehensive services. With sufficient time, we arrange alternatives to incarceration for women who are facing criminal charges related to addiction, prostitution, and violations of probation and parole. Power Inside conducts assessments, brokers community resources, and then presents treatment plans in court proceedings in conjunction with their attorney, usually a public defender. A typical treatment plan includes drug treatment, health services, and intensive case management. Advocacy in criminal court proceedings is necessary in order to bring attention to issues often overlooked such as women's abuse histories, family and community ties, and treatment options as judges weigh whether incarceration is warranted in each case.

In the community–Power Inside maintains a drop-in center for women transitioning to the community after prison and jail and for those seeking respite from street and shelter life. Women are offered a safe atmosphere to make telephone calls, socialize, and receive case management and peer support. Tutoring and support groups are also available to women who come to the office. Staff accompanies women to appointments and advocates with other organizations in order to offset the many barriers they face. We also provide food, bus tokens, clothing and assist with obtaining identification, housing, job training and healthcare.

On the street–Power Inside community health outreach workers provide services directly on the streets–offering peer counseling, hygiene supplies, condoms, blankets, crisis intervention and accompaniments to emergency rooms, needle exchange, or clinics. Street outreach extends our continuum to homeless women who are cycling through jail who are less likely to access other community-based services. We work with women on their turf and on an individual, network and community level to facilitate positive change and increase access to public health systems.

Focus on families–Power Inside recognizes the mother-child connection as fundamental to the health and healing of families. We offer support to incarcerated and formerly incarcerated mothers who wish to strengthen relationships, heal from separation, and advocate for the well-being of their family. As mothers re-build family connections, we extend our holistic services to their children, child caregivers, and partners. Once a mother is incarcerated, caring for children often becomes paramount to the extended family in an attempt to prevent children from entering the foster care system. Little support exists for these caregivers who provide for the food, housing and nurturing of children. Costs associated with the mother's incarceration, such as collect calls, transportation for visits, and postage add to financial burdens. The emotional toll on children, caregivers, and incarcerated mothers carries a devastating impact. Children's lives are disrupted by the uncertainty and social stigma related to having an incarcerated parent. Incarcerated mothers try to fulfill their parenting responsibilities from prison. Others try to protect children from shame and conceal their incarceration–leaving children to feel abandoned by their mothers. Power Inside meets with the extended family of incarcerated mothers in their home to offer support and encouragement. If children are in foster care we facilitate between family members and with mothers in jail or prison. It is also necessary to advocate for families needing assistance with public entitlements, housing authorities, the courts, and juvenile services.

Focus on young adult women–Young incarcerated women have complex life experiences that place them at particular risk. Power Inside offers a support group to young women (ages 16-25) at the Maryland Correctional Institution for Women. Abuse, street violence, drugs and alcohol, poverty, and community instability are dominant themes in their lives from an early age. Peers 'on the streets' become their primary source of social support, often pushing them deeper into a life of risk and violence. Involvement with abusive partners makes the pursuit of a life free from violence more difficult. By the time they reach the adult correctional system, they often have had longstanding contact with the foster care and juvenile justice systems. The young women's group, "Keeping It Real," gives them a place to develop conflict resolution, leadership, critical thinking, communication, and negotiation skills in a positive and culturally specific atmosphere.

CHALLENGES

Power Inside is faced with both internal and external challenges that we must address in order to reach our program goals. Women fall between the cracks due to the scarcity of family and health services, safe and affordable housing, and economic opportunity available to women cycling through the criminal justice system. Our limitations require us to rely on collaborations with existing programs that do not have a specific focus on women transitioning from incarceration to the community. For some women we are able to locate residential drug treatment or supportive housing and witness the powerful transformation as they reclaim their lives and reunite with their families. But many are also discharged from jail at night; they are homeless, with no coat, no money for a phone call, no identification, and no bus fare. Others leave incarceration and, without options, return to abusive relationships. In the frequent scenario of "no place to go," a hierarchy of needs continually brings our focus back to attending to women's most basic need to simply survive. We dedicate resources to sustaining homeless women and families day-to-day using outreach, hospitality, food, referrals, and ongoing crisis intervention. At times, they build the self-advocacy skills needed to access mainstream services. Others give up as we seek shelter or drug treatment for them. Although we may stave off a downward spiral for women individually, we are continually confronted with the systemic change needed to truly prevent women from being re-incarcerated.

FUTURE DIRECTION

Power Inside's future will be determined by our ability to build capacity, secure funding, and successfully articulate the needs of women we encounter. We currently are in a development and evaluation process to capture outcomes and document program efficacy. Findings from the WINDOW Study will be used to support our advocacy seeking policy changes that ensure that women are given a fair chance and humane choices as they attempt to reenter the community after release from jail. The difficult work ahead will require Power Inside to continue to foster innovative relationships with the systems and institutions that intersect women's lives in order to effectively intervene with and advocate for them. As the program becomes more established, it is important that we retain our foundation as a grassroots community-based organization in order to honor the contributions made by women who have been directly impacted by gender-based violence and the criminal justice system. As we have learned, our short history and success can be wholly attributed to women who have guided the growth and development of Power Inside, not as consumers of services, but as leaders in envisioning families and communities that possess safety, health and justice.

REFERENCES

Bloom, B., Owens, B., & Covington, S. (2003). *Gender responsive strategies: Research, practice and guiding principles for women offenders* (Publication Number 99D03GIL4). National Institute of Corrections. Crenshaw, K. (1991). Mapping the margins: Intersectionality, identity politics, and violence against women of color. *Stanford Law Review, 43*, 1241-1299.

Freire, P. (1972). *Pedagogy of the oppressed.* New York, NY: Continuum.

Marlatt, G. A. (1996). Harm reduction: come as you are. *Addictive Behaviors, 21*, 779-788.

McLean, R., Robarge, J., & Sherman, S. (2005). *The WINDOW study–release from jail: moment of crisis or window of opportunity for female detainees in Baltimore city?* Baltimore, MD: Power Inside.

Miller, J. B. (1976). *Toward a new psychology of women.* Boston, MA: Beacon Press.

Miller, W. R., & Rollnick, S. (1991) *Motivational interviewing: preparing people for change.* New York, NY: Guilford Press.

Prochaska, J. O., & DiClemente, C. C. (1984). *The transtheoretical approach: crossing traditional boundaries of treatment.* Homewood, IL: Dow Jones-Irwin.

United States Department of Justice (n.d.). 2002. Civil rights division special litigations section investigative findings: Baltimore city detention center. Retrieved July 30, 2006 from http://www.usdoj.gov/crt/split/documents/baltimore_findings_let.htm.

Wilkerson, J. L. (2002). *The essense of being real: relational peer support for men and women who have experienced trauma.* Baltimore, MD: Sidran Press.

doi:10.1300/J012v17n02_08

Defining a Research Agenda on Women and Justice in the Age of Mass Incarceration

Jeremy Travis

SUMMARY. Although the issues of women involved in the criminal justice system, the impact incarceration of women has on children, and the specific issues formerly incarcerated women face upon reentry into the community are regarded as critical areas of research, this paper focuses on issues that lie at the penumbra of the broader discussion of women and justice and fall under the general heading of "collateral damage" experienced in the modern era of mass incarceration. Specifically, two topics are addressed: first, the impact of our justice policies on women living in communities that experience high concentrations of arrest, removal, incarceration and reentry; and second, the burdens borne by women in connection with the reentry process. doi:10.1300/J012v17n02_09 *[Article copies available for a fee from The Haworth Document Delivery Service: 1-800-HAWORTH. E-mail address: <docdelivery@haworthpress.com> Website: <http://www.HaworthPress.com> © 2006 by The Haworth Press, Inc. All rights reserved.]*

KEYWORDS. Mass incarceration, criminal justice, reintegration, gender imbalance, substance abuse, women-centered, high incarceration communities

Jeremy Travis is President, John Jay College of Criminal Justice.

[Haworth co-indexing entry note]: "Defining a Research Agenda on Women and Justice in the Age of Mass Incarceration." Travis, Jeremy. Co-published simultaneously in *Women & Criminal Justice* (The Haworth Press, Inc.) Vol. 17, No. 2/3, 2006, pp. 127-136; and: *Drugs, Women, and Justice: Roles of the Criminal Justice System for Drug-Affected Women* (ed: James A. Swartz, Patricia O'Brien, and Arthur J. Lurigio) The Haworth Press, Inc., 2006, pp. 127-136. Single or multiple copies of this article are available for a fee from The Haworth Document Delivery Service [1-800-HAWORTH, 9:00 a.m. - 5:00 p.m. (EST). E-mail address: docdelivery@haworthpress.com].

COMMUNITY LEVEL EFFECTS:
THE "GENDER IMBALANCE"

Over the past generation, we have more than quadrupled the per capita rate of incarceration in this country. For fifty years, from 1920 to
the early 1970's, we had a stable rate of incarceration–about 110 per
100,000. Then, beginning in 1972, that rate started to rise, and has risen
every year until it now exceeds 486 per 100,000 (Harrison & Beck,
2005). Some academics have coined the phrase "mass incarceration" as
an apt description for the current state of justice in America (Drucker
2002; Mauer & Chesney-Lind, 2002; Pattillo, Weiman, & Western,
2004).

It is clear that we have embarked on an unprecedented social experiment, basically asking, "What will be the effects of a quadrupling of the
rate of incarceration in our democracy?" One thing we know for certain:
these effects are not equally distributed across the country. Rather, they
are felt acutely in a small number of communities, typically communities of color in urban America that are simultaneously struggling with
concentrated disadvantage along any number of dimensions, including
poor health care, inadequate educational systems, high rates of unemployment, and disproportionate rates of crime.

We know another thing for certain, and that is that the high rates of
incarceration disproportionately involve men, not women. Although
the numbers of women in our nation's prisons are certainly increasing,
the reality is that most prisoners–about 90 percent–are men.

The interaction of these three phenomena–record high levels of imprisonment, concentrated in a small number of communities of color,
disproportionately involving men–has created a new, unprecedented
social reality. Several examples paint a more specific picture of this reality. According to research conducted in East New York, a high incarceration community in Brooklyn, New York, on the blocks experiencing
the highest rates of incarceration, one in eight men between the ages of
16 and 44 will be arrested and sent to jail or prison each year (Cadora &
Swartz, 1999). According to a study published in Chicago by the North
Lawndale Employment Network, approximately 70 percent of the men
in North Lawndale have a criminal record (McKean & Raphael, 2002).
Clearly, in neighborhoods such as these, growing up male most likely
involves one or more experiences in the criminal justice system. These
community-level effects can also be understood by citing a troubling
national statistic: according to the Bureau of Justice Statistics, an African

American male today faces a 30 percent likelihood that he will spend at least a year of his life in prison (Bonczar, 2003).

This sobering new social reality should command significant attention from the research community; of particular interest is the impact of high rates of male incarceration on the relationships between young men and young women in these communities of high rates of incarceration. My thinking on this topic has been particularly influenced by the work of Donald Braman, an anthropologist who assessed the impact of mass incarceration on family and community life in Washington, DC. His research, published in a book entitled "Doing Time on the Outside" (University of Michigan Press, 2004), documents a profound impact on the gender relationships in those communities. The starting point of his analysis is the documentation of a "gender imbalance"–simply put, a shortage of men. This shortage is both a shortage in a quantitative sense–there are fewer men compared to women–and in the qualitative sense–many of the men who are available are less "marketable," to use a crass metric, because of their involvement in the criminal justice system.

Braman's research in Washington, DC illustrates the dimensions of the "gender imbalance," though arguably, his findings could likely be replicated in many American cities. According to Braman, more than 75 percent of African-American men in Washington can expect to be incarcerated in their lifetime. Half of the women in the nation's capital live in communities with low incarceration rates. In those communities, there are about 94 men for every 100 women. For the rest of the women, living in neighborhoods with higher rates of incarceration, the ratio is about 80 men for every 100 women. But, 10 percent of the women in Washington live in neighborhoods with extremely high rates of incarceration, where more than 12 percent of the men are behind bars. In these neighborhoods, there are fewer than 62 men for every 100 women.

The research questions suggested by these data and anecdotes are quite profound. What is the nature of dating relationships in these communities? How will the notion of male and female identity be influenced by the realities of the gender imbalance? How will patterns of family formation be affected? How will the levels of households headed by women change in the years to come? How has the influence of peer networks changed as more men are involved in the criminal justice system? How will the relationship between women and the workplace change in years to come, assuming that families will become even more dependent on their income in the future? How will the accumulation of family wealth be affected?

Recent research provides some insights into these questions. Braman found that the gender imbalance translates into large numbers of father-less families in communities with high rates of incarceration. In Washington, fathers are absent from half of the families. But in communities with the highest male incarceration rates–about 12 percent–more than three-quarters of the families had a father absent. Incarceration also alters the relationships between the men and women who are not incarcerated. In her research on the marriage patterns of low-income mothers, Edin (2000) found that the decision to marry (or remarry) depends, in part, on the economic prospects, social respectability, and reliability of potential husbands–attributes that are adversely affected by imprisonment. Low marriage rates, in turn, affect the life courses of men who have been imprisoned, reducing their likelihood of desistance from criminal activity. Thus, the communities with the highest rates of incarceration are caught in what Western, Lopoo, and McLanahan (2004, 21) call the "high-crime/low-marriage equilibrium." In these communities, women "will be understandably averse to marriage because their potential partners bring few social or economic benefits to the table. Men, who remain unmarried or unattached to stable households, are likely to continue their criminal involvement."

But there is clearly much more to learn about the impact of mass incarceration on women in high incarceration communities. A research agenda is needed that is woman-centered, not offender-centered, and not even woman-offender-centered. The era of mass incarceration has profoundly changed the dynamics of human development, male-female relationships, and the roles of women, and we need a research frame that captures these broad effects. For policy-making purposes, there is considerable urgency to the development of this agenda. If one assumes–and I regretfully have concluded this is a reasonable assumption, based on the politics of criminal justice policy (Travis, 2005)–that our current high rates of incarceration will continue for the foreseeable future, then we have crossed a Rubicon of sorts that will affect generations to come.

There are no exact parallels in our history. Certainly we can learn some lessons from studies of the impact of the welfare system on families in the African American and Latino communities. There are some similarities to the reality just described–in both, we witness the perverse financial incentives that undermine family life, the intrusion of government authority into family matters, including the relationships between men and women and parents and children, and the creation of states of dependency on governmental support. Perhaps we can learn some lessons from research on relationships between men and women and the functioning of families in countries engaged in war or experiencing civil strife. We have little understanding of the psychological impact of imprisonment, but we can document elevated levels of post-traumatic stress disorder among returning prisoners. Researchers could explore the similarities with the experiences of returning soldiers, who display high rates of divorce, alcoholism and substance abuse, and ruptured and violent intimate relationships.

In short, as we seek a better understanding of the community level effects of incarceration, we should focus squarely on the changing nature of male-female relationships, starting with an understanding of the "gender imbalance," and extending to include research on the developmental implications for the upcoming generation of young boys and girls.

STRESS ON THE FAMILIAL SUPPORT SYSTEM

Closely related to the research agenda on the "gender imbalance" is a research agenda on the impact of mass incarceration on the support system for the individuals, mostly men, who are arrested, incarcerated, and then return to the communities just described. Again, we are exploring the penumbra of incarceration's effects–the collateral damage that is a consequence of our current justice policies.

The social network most directly affected by an individual's incarceration is predominantly a female network. The most clear cut data supporting this assertion describe the network that cares for children of incarcerated parents. Two-thirds of incarcerated mothers are the sole custodial parent before incarceration. By contrast, about 40 percent of fathers in prison reported living with both their children and their children's mothers. When the custodial parent is incarcerated, a new caregiver enters the picture. These new arrangements reflect the gender of the prisoner. More than half of the children who lived with their mother went to live with a grandparent when their mother was sent to prison. But nearly 90 percent of children who lived with their father lived with their mother during the father's incarceration. For incarcerated mothers, 10 percent have children placed in foster care, compared with only 2 percent of incarcerated fathers (Travis, Cincotta & Solomon, 2003). Clearly, when Mom or Dad is incarcerated, a familial network typically led by a woman–whether the child's mother, a mother surrogate, or a grandmother–rallies to care for the child while the parent is incarcerated.

We do not calculate the costs of this new burden on already overburdened families when we calculate the costs of incarceration. But these costs are as real as the price of constructing new prisons. In essence, we have placed new parenting burdens on a large number of women in communities experiencing high rates of incarceration and we provide little or no assistance to them as they shoulder the responsibility of raising the next generation. So, an immediate research task is to document the extent of the new burden–how are these women coping, what new life choices are they making, how are the children faring, and what are the positive and negative effects of this new task assigned to existing social networks?

But the burdens assumed by these networks extend far beyond added childcare responsibilities. First and foremost are the added costs of maintaining contact with the family member in prison. Donald Braman tells the story of Lilly, a Washington DC resident whose son, Anthony, is incarcerated in Ohio (Braman, 2002). She can only manage monthly visits to see her son, bringing her daughter, Anthony's sister. For each two-day trip, she spends between $150 and $200 for car rental, food, and a motel. Added to these costs are the money orders to supplement his inmate account and the care packages she is allowed to send twice a year. She also pays about $100 a month for the collect calls he places. She does all this on a fixed income of $530 a month.

This story is one of hundreds we could tell in high incarceration communities. The era of mass incarceration is, in effect, draining income from poor families, causing these families to make painful and harmful choices between competing claims for the family's financial resources. The family member in prison suffers. The rest of the family suffers. And, in the case of the collect calls, for which the surcharge is typically collected by the phone company and passed along to the prison system as part of their contract, family resources are in essence being used to subsidize the costs of imprisonment.

We should then add to our list of research priorities an economic assessment of the impact of incarceration on prisoners' families. It is so ironic that political leaders, particularly those on the conservative end of the spectrum, pay homage to the American family, and decry the weakening of the family in poor communities, yet fail to recognize the destructive effects of mass incarceration on precisely the same families they avowedly seek to strengthen. These families were never intended to be punished by our criminal justice system but are punished nonetheless.

Families also shoulder new burdens at the time a prisoner returns home. Thanks to research conducted by the Urban Institute in its *Returning*

Home study, we now have a much better understanding of the role of families and particularly the role of female family members–in the re-entry process. According to this research, nearly half (45 percent) of the men leaving prison in Illinois and returning to Chicago had high expectations of family support after their release–both emotional and tangible support. These expectations were realized and exceeded. After release, 59 percent received income from a spouse, family, or friends, and nearly all (92 percent) reported that someone in their family provided financial support. About three quarters said they expected to live with their families after they left prison, but when surveyed between four and eight months after release, 88 percent were living with their family.

Perhaps not surprisingly, given the critical role of family in the release process, formerly incarcerated individuals credited family with an important role in their success in staying out of prison. And their appreciation grew over time. Prior to release, 58 percent of the returning prisoners interviewed said that family would be important in helping avoid prison. After release, family support was cited by 71 percent of the respondents (LaVigne, Visher & Castro, 2004).

The *Returning Home* study documents another kind of strain on families in communities of high rates of incarceration. They are performing a critical social function–the reintegration of large numbers of returning prisoners, most of whom are men. From a research perspective, we need to develop a better understanding of these social strains on the family. More specifically, because women most often head the family units and the reintegrating prisoners are most often men, we need to understand this phenomenon through gender-specific analysis. And, because strong families are associated with reduced rates of rearrest following prison, we should, from a policy perspective, find ways to strengthen families so they can better perform this critical social function.

THE BURDENS OF PRISONER REINTEGRATION

In recent years, there has been a substantial level of policy ferment, programmatic innovation, and legislative activity focusing on ways to improve outcomes for the 630,000 individuals who return home from our state and federal prisons each year. This represents an important development in the history of justice reform efforts and, for those of us involved in the early days of these initiatives, is very gratifying. One of the key elements of the reentry reform agenda is increasing the involvement of the families of returning prisoners. In my description of the "principles of effective reentry," I have called for "strengthening the concentric circles of support," particularly the families of the formerly incarcerated (Travis, 2005).

Research from New York City illustrates both the potential and the risk associated with this strategy. A demonstration project launched by the Vera Institute of Justice, called *La Bodega de la Familia*, was designed to answer an important question, namely whether providing support to the family members of former prisoners who had histories of drug addiction could help them in overcoming their addictions. The program was striking in its simplicity. The intervention was called "family case management." The idea was to utilize the strengths of families to influence the behavior of a family member who is under criminal justice supervision. The working hypothesis was that interventions that would strengthen families–for example, giving them access to crisis intervention, helping them develop effective interventions regarding drug use, preventing eviction of the family from public housing, providing counseling, etc.–would reduce the drug use and criminal behavior of the family member under criminal justice supervision.

But the results did not quite meet the planners' expectations. First the good news: the levels of drug use among the target population did in fact decline. While 86 percent of the participants had used at least one substance during the month prior to joining the program, this proportion declined to 50 percent after six months in the program–a statistically significant reduction greater than that found in a comparison group. These positive results were achieved even though there was NO increase in the levels of participation in treatment programs among the subject population (Sullivan et al., 2002). So, on one level, the program was a success–supporting families could indeed lead to reduced drug use. (Interestingly, these positive findings on reductions in drug use did not translate into similar findings on recidivism rates. While program participants were also about half as likely to be arrested and convicted for a new offense as members of the comparison group, the numbers were too small to draw statistically sound conclusions.)

Yet these positive results came with a cost. The research found that–notwithstanding improvements in their services, support networks, and health status–the families participating in the La Bodega program reported higher rates of emotional problems and stress than at the beginning of the program. The evaluators suggested a possible explanation: "Perhaps as a consequence of having the issues surrounding drug abuse out on the table and having to deal with them openly, the La Bodega users and their family members experienced increased conflict in their relationships" (Sullivan et al., 2002, 51).

The findings from the evaluation of *La Bodega de la Familia* provide the proper frame for my recommendations for research priorities when we examine the intersection of the topics of drugs, women and justice. When we assess the consequences of the historic rise in levels of incarceration, we should not limit our analysis to those who are imprisoned. As important as it is to understand the consequences of the increase in women in prison, and the intersection of drug abuse and the war on drugs on women, the ripple effects of this grand social experiment are far reaching and our research agenda must be equally far-reaching. We need to understand the profound realignment of relationships between men and women, boys and girls in communities of high justice system penetration. We need to understand the costs borne by prisoners' social networks, networks in which women figure prominently. And, to the extent we seek to promote positive reentry outcomes for record numbers of prisoners, most of whom are men, we should not lightly call upon these same women to bear the added social responsibility for successful reintegration. Their burdens are already heavy; they are already unwitting partners in holding our communities together while hundreds of thousands of men, and a smaller number of women, are temporarily exiled into our nation's prisons, only to return home again. These women do indeed represent invaluable community assets, and we should support them as they play new roles thrust upon them by the era of mass incarceration.

REFERENCES

Austin, J., & Irwin, J. (2001). *It's about time: America's imprisonment binge (3rd ed)*. Belmont, CA: Wadsworth.

Bonczar, T. P. (2003). Prevalence of imprisonment in the U.S. population, 1974-2001. (U.S. DOJ Publication No. NCJ 197976). Washington, DC: U.S. Government Printing Office.

Braman, D. (2002). Families and incarceration. In M. Mauer & M. Chesney-Lind (Eds.), *Invisible punishment: The collateral consequences of mass imprisonment*, (pp. 117-135). New York: The New Press.

Braman, D. (2004). *Doing time on the outside: Incarceration and family life in urban America*. Ann Arbor: University of Michigan Press.

Cadora, E., & Charles, S. (1999). *The community justice project at the center for alter native sentencing and employment services (CASES)*. For more information see http://www.communityjusticeproject.org.

Drucker, E. (2002). Population impact of mass incarceration under New York's Rockefeller drug laws: An analysis of years of life lost. *Journal of Urban Health, 79*(3), 434-435.

Edin, K. (2000). Few good men: Why poor mothers don't marry or remarry. *The American Prospect, 11*(4), 26-31.

Harrison, P. M., & Beck, A. J. (2005). Prison and jail inmates at midyear 2003. (U.S. DOJ Publication No. NCJ 208801). Washington, DC: U.S. Government Printing Office.

La Vigne, N. G., Visher, C., & Castro, J. (2004). *Chicago prisoners' experiences returning home.* Washington, DC: The Urban Institute.

Mauer, M., & Chesney-Lind, M. (Eds.) (2002). *Invisible punishment: The collateral consequences of mass imprisonment.* New York: The New Press.

McKean, L., & Raphael, J. (2002). *Drugs, crime and consequences: Arrests and incarceration in North Lawndale.* Chicago: North Lawndale Employment Network.

Pattillo, M., Weiman, D., & Western, B. (Eds.) (2004). *Imprisoning America: The social effects of mass incarceration.* New York: Russell Sage Foundation.

Sullivan, E., Mino, M., Nelson, K., & Pope, J. (2002). *Families as a resource in recovery from drug abuse: An evaluation of La Bodega de la Familia.* New York: Vera Institute of Justice.

Travis, J. (2005). *But they all come back: Facing the challenges of prisoner reentry.* Washington, DC: The Urban Institute Press.

Travis, J., Cincotta, E. M., & Solomon, A. (2003). *Families left behind: The hidden cost of incarceration and reentry.* Washington, DC: The Urban Institute.

Western, B., Lopoo, L. M., & McLanahan, S. (2004). Incarceration and the bonds between parents in fragile families. In M. Patillo, D. Weiman, & B. Western (Eds.), *Imprisoning America: The social effects of mass incarceration,* (pp. 21-45). New York: Russell Sage Foundation.

doi:10.1300/J012v17n02_09

Women and Drug Use:
The Case for a Justice Analysis

Beth E. Richie

SUMMARY. Extensive data link women's use of drugs and their subsequent involvement in illegal activity to their growing involvement with the criminal justice system. Although research has established causal factors and consequences for drug use among women, these factors do not take into account the fundamental social injustices that also contribute to drug use among women, including interactions with social institutions, social sigma, and punitive public policy. This paper discusses the importance of developing theoretical frameworks and measures for assessing social (in)justice that would allow for it to be operationalized, generalized, and tested for validity in order to help explain what justice is and how injustice works as a broader causal mechanism in the growing problem of women and drug use. doi:10.1300/J012v17n02_10 *[Article copies available for a fee from The Haworth Document Delivery Service: 1-800-HAWORTH. E-mail address: <docdelivery@haworthpress.com> Website: <http://www.HaworthPress.com> © 2006 by The Haworth Press, Inc. All rights reserved.]*

KEYWORDS. Women, drug use, criminal justice system, social justice, social injustice, marginalization, causal factors, disadvantaged, social stigma

Beth E. Richie is Professor in the Departments of African American Studies and Criminology, Law and Justice, University of Illinois at Chicago.

[Haworth co-indexing entry note]: "Women and Drug Use: The Case for a Justice Analysis." Richie, Beth E. Co-published simultaneously in *Women & Criminal Justice* (The Haworth Press, Inc.) Vol. 17, No. 2/3, 2006, pp. 137-143; and: *Drugs, Women, and Justice: Roles of the Criminal Justice System for Drug-Affected Women* (ed: James A. Swartz, Patricia O'Brien, and Arthur J. Lurigio) The Haworth Press, Inc., 2006, pp. 137-143. Single or multiple copies of this article are available for a fee from The Haworth Document Delivery Service [1-800-HAWORTH, 9:00 a.m. - 5:00 p.m. (EST). E-mail address: docdelivery@haworthpress.com].

INTRODUCTION

There is extensive data that links women's use of drugs and their sub-sequent involvement in illegal activity resulting in their growing pres-ence in the population who are incarcerated or otherwise under the surveillance and control of the criminal legal system in this country. Scholars, policy makers, intervention specialists, criminal justice pro-fessionals, advocates and community members alike understand that this is one of the most serious problems facing society today, as evi-denced by morbidity and mortality rates, incarceration statistics, data from child protective services and other bureaucratic institutions and court records. Moreover, anecdotal evidence from neighborhood level analyses attests to the pressing nature of the problem of women and sub-stance abuse.

A review of the literature reveals several epistemological trends in the data that describe the problem. One body of research looks at indi-vidual level psychological analyses of causation. Other studies attempt to recognize the link between substance abuse and other social prob-lems such as poverty and violence. There are important accounts of the ways that certain groups of women are disproportionately affected by the problem and significant evaluation research of program effective-ness and model intervention strategies.

Much of this is very good research that stands up to the most ambi-tious standards of scientific rigor; the research questions are good ones, the methodological approaches are sound, the samples are appropriate, and the analytic strategies are well thought out. In the aggregate, the conclusions from this body of work illuminate many of the factors that are important to the understanding about women and their drug abuse in contemporary society. These conclusions could be summarized in the following way.

Women use drugs for a number of reasons. While some of the causal factors have been established as similar to the reasons that men use drugs, there are particular risk factors that pre-dispose women to sub-stance abuse, including relational subordination and exposure to inti-mate partner violence. Another area of gender difference is the effect and consequences of drug abuse. Pharmacological research has estab-lished that certain drugs have a unique physiological effect on women and social analyses reveal that society's response to the problem of sub-stance abuse is, in many ways, more severe. In addition, it has been shown that the process of recovery for women is different and that programs need to take what is called a "gender-specific approach" to treatment.

Finally, almost all studies have indicated that women of color from low-income communities are disproportionately represented in the population of women affected by illegal drug use in the United States.

This summative picture of the research findings could be stated another way. Consider the following assessment: Gender violence with its root causes in male domination, predispose women to substance abuse, as does economic marginalization and persistent poverty. These and other issues that affect women's sense of self worth–like degrading interactions with social institutions, social stigma and punitive public policy–further increase their risk of substance abuse and the concomitant consequences. Institutional neglect is also indicated as a major risk factor, and given racial and class hierarchy, it follows that women of color from low-income communities are most likely to experience the negative consequences of substance abuse; their treatment needs are not addressed and they are sanctioned by the criminal legal system most harshly.

The two versions of the summary and the differential language used to describe the research findings represent more than semantic differences. On the one hand, the focus on individual pathology and the "empiricist" assessments can lead scholars, policy makers and intervention specialists to direct attention (and blame) and resources (including law enforcement apparatus) to individuals in a way that is harmful rather than helpful. In the second version of the problem, the larger concerns become paramount, bringing into focus issues such as poverty, racism, inequality, and gender oppression, which are typically outside the domain of study.

The second narrative also enables a justice perspective by reframing the research questions. It allows for the creation of a set of recommendations about how research on women and drugs could serve a broad social justice agenda goal as well as the goal of advancing the specific knowledge about women and crime. The re-framing is built on the following five assertions. First, it is important to include the concept of justice as a theoretical area of inquiry when looking at the issue of women and substance abuse. Second, it is important to include questions about experiences of injustice among the variables considered when the causes and the consequences of substance abuse are measured in studies of women and substance abuse, particularly with regard to questions of desistance. Third, as research findings are translated into questions of intervention, it is essential that work addressing injustices appears in the array of services provided. Finally, researchers must ask how public policy can be refocused to include more than punishment so that it is reoriented towards the re-distribution of power and resources to meet the goals of justice and equality.

Prior to elaboration on these issues, it is important to explain that in this paper, I am using the term "justice" to signify the range of conditions that would expand opportunity for those who have been constrained by their social position or lack of access to institutional privileges. The concept as I use it includes creating a set of circumstances where disadvantaged groups or individuals who experience injustice are compensated for their plight. Analytically, it means that our understanding of social problems includes the ways that disenfranchisement contributes to individual pathology and social deviance and the role of institutions and the state in creating opportunities for redress. Justice, in this sense, works to both validate the sense that macro variables play a role in the creation of individual pathology and treatment of injustice is corrective at the level of broader social forces. An analysis that points to the need for advancing justice as part of the solution to a social problem like drug abuse by women focuses attention on the role that the state and its institutions play in the creation of conditions that lead to individual dysfunction. Intervention is aimed at restoring rights, creating opportunity and strengthening the social position of those who suffer the most in contemporary society; as in the case of women who use drugs.

JUSTICE AS A RESEARCH QUESTION

When we think of justice in this way, a new set of research questions emerges as significant. In addition to the very important work of exploring the link between women's substance abuse and conditions in their family of origin, the role of their peers in risk-taking behavior, women's individual reactions to stress or other individual factors that predispose them to the risk of substance abuse, asking questions about the role of injustice opens a broader area for researchers to explore. Such questions might include attention to the role that economic marginalization played in women's involvement in the illegal drug trade, the role that gender oppression played in women's use of drugs with their partners and the role that institutional policy played in their inability to comply with treatment protocols. Exploring these and related areas would allow researchers to expose the role that macro level forces play in women's substance abuse–not as a way to diminish or compete with the importance of individual characteristics–but as a way to look for additional causal factors.

JUSTICE AS AN ANALYTIC VARIABLE

When justice is included in the research questions and hypotheses, it can then be treated as an analytic category. Here I am not only suggesting that an operationalized notion of justice be included on data collection instruments (survey instruments, questionnaires or interview schedules), but that researchers define and quantify the concept in such a way that participant's responses and/or field observations can be interpreted by researchers as issues of justice *even if* they are not defined in precisely those terms by the women substance abusers who make up the sample being studied. In the same way that depression is measured, for example, injustice could be operationalized in concrete terms that were generalizable and tested for validity. It must be recognized that there is some important literature that attempts to quantify related terms, such as "empowerment" or "self efficacy," however in the research on substance abuse, an analytic category that includes elements of justice is under-developed. To remedy this would be an ambitious scientific project, however I assert that without standardization, discussion of the role that injustice plays in women's substance abuse will remain at the level of rhetoric rather than "social science."

JUSTICE AS A DESISTANCE FACTOR

The extent to which reallocating resources, changing institutional policies, restoring individual rights or other efforts towards decreasing social inequality will lead to reduction or desistance of substance abuse in women remains an empirical question. Moreover, the relationship between social arrangements that disadvantage certain groups of women and their concentration in the populations of substance abusers has not received much research attention except as a descriptive reality. I argue that this level of discussion is not only inadequate, it is dangerous. That is, to say that "most of the women in this study were women of color and/or poor" (as most reports of research findings on women and substance abuse do) leaves some readers feeling like that is neither an analytic problem nor a political one. It is stated as a fact rather than as a critical research question. Researchers interested in justice will want to understand (1) *why* that is the case and (2) what role the *social conditions that create injustice* had in the creation of the problem and society's response to it. Here a theoretical discussion the likes of which have been advanced by feminists of color and critical race theorists is warranted.

JUSTICE AS AN INTERVENTION PROGRAM

In addition to challenging taken-for-granted over representation of women of color among illicit substance users and those more often sanctioned by the criminal justice system, and prompting new areas of inquiry, introducing justice as a research question allows for a new set of possibilities around intervention research. What would an intervention program that included social justice in its program goals look like? Who or what would be the "target" of the intervention? What activities would be included in the therapeutic menus offered to those who are suffering? What would the role of punishment or other state sanctions be in responding to the problem? How would program success be measured? These types of questions are being asked by a growing cohort of scholars/practitioners who are interested in advancing a different kind of feminist intervention on problems that marginalized groups of women face. These include programs that build community organizing skills, which engage so-called "clients" in action research that is aimed towards social transformation as opposed to only providing social services. The field of women's substance abuse treatment research could benefit from and build on this work were it to embrace the notion of justice research. Multi-method studies and analytical strategies that privilege those who are most affected as the people who validate knowledge are indicated. In addition, studies that look at resistance as well as protective factors would also serve the goal of advancing understanding of the relationship between women, drug abuse and justice.

JUSTICE AS PUBLIC POLICY

The criminal legal system has, in a sense, hijacked the notion of justice to such an extent that feminist researchers and other scholars interested in exploring questions of substance abuse and women have avoided mentioning (let alone engaging in serious scientific debates about) the concept. I am arguing here that it is time to re-position the notion of justice as a key aspect of women's health and healing from drug abuse and other manifestations of social injustice. I am suggesting that we seriously consider questions of injustice as causal factors and that we develop scientific instruments and theoretical paradigms that help to explain what justice is and how injustice works as a causal mechanism. Such an endeavor would enable scientific research that results in findings that could not only be integrated into treatment programs, but would point to other avenues of desistance work. Lastly, public policy could emerge that is more effective and humane, and that has longer-term results than the current agenda of sanctions and disenfranchisement, which the current research invokes.

We know a lot about the micro, individual causes and consequences of substance abuse among women. What we have yet to understand, is the link between these micro level issues and women's experience in the broader social sphere related to their disadvantaged social position, their limited access to resources and the ways that institutions fail them. Public policy that is aimed at changing that situation (as opposed to changing or sanctioning women themselves) is likely to be more effective in resolving the problem of substance abuse. At the very least, I am arguing that equal attention needs to be given to this assertion in our research agenda.

Index